Spotlight on Young Children

Observation & Assessment

Volume 2

Hilary Seitz EDITOR

National Association for the Education of Young Children
Washington, DC

naeyc®

National Association for the Education of Young Children

1401 H Street NW, Suite 600
Washington, DC 20005
202-232-8777 • 800-424-2460
NAEYC.org

NAEYC Books

Senior Director, Publishing & Content Development
Susan Friedman

Director, Books
Dana Battaglia

Senior Editor
Holly Bohart

Editor II
Rossella Procopio

Senior Creative Design Manager
Charity Coleman

Senior Creative Design Specialist
Gillian Frank

Publishing Business Operations Manager
Francine Markowitz

Through its publications program, the National Association for the Education of Young Children (NAEYC) provides a forum for discussion of major issues and ideas in the early childhood field, with the hope of provoking thought and promoting professional growth. The views expressed or implied in this book are not necessarily those of the Association.

The following selections were previously published in the specified issues of *Teaching Young Children*: M. Macy and S.J. Bagnato, "Authentic and Meaningful Developmental Screening in Early Childhood," Fall 2022, and C. Scott-Little, with K.L. Reschke, "Foundations of Assessment for Preschool Settings," Fall 2022.

The following selections were previously published in the specified issues of *Young Children*: E. Regenstein, M.C. Connors, R. Romero-Jurado, and J. Weiner, "Effective Kindergarten Readiness Assessments: Influencing Policy, Informing Instruction, and Creating Joyful Classrooms," March 2018; D. LeeKeenan and I.C. Ponte, "Meaningful Assessment and Documentation: How Directors Can Support Teaching and Learning," November 2018; J.L. Gooch, "Enhancing Toddlers' Communication Skills: Partnerships with Speech-Language Pathologists," March 2019; C.C. Bates, S.M. Schenck, and H.J. Hoover, "Anecdotal Records: Practical Strategies for Taking Meaningful Notes," July 2019; C. Catlett and E.P. Soukakou, "Assessing Opportunities to Support Each Child: 12 Practices for Quality Inclusion," July 2019; S.A. Roller, E.P. Cunningham, and K.A. Marin, "Photographs and Learning Progressions: Supports for Intentional Assessment and Instruction in Mathematics," July 2019; C.M. Snyder and H.P. Delgado, "Unlocking the Potential of Data-Driven Coaching: Child Assessment Evidence as a Guide for Informing Instructional Practices," July 2019; C.G. Coogle, E.R. Lakey, J.R. Ottley, J.A. Brown, and M.K. Romano, "Embedded Learning Opportunities for Children with and Without Disabilities," Winter 2021; N.N. Jones, A.T. Fowler, and J.K. Adair, "Assessing Agency in Learning Contexts: A First, Critical Step to Assessing Children," Spring 2023; R. Parlakian, "Bringing Observation and Documentation to Life in Infant and Toddler Settings," Spring 2023; and H. Seitz, "Authentic Assessment: A Strengths-Based Approach to Making Thinking, Learning, and Development Visible," Spring 2023.

"Improving Practice" on page 70 is excerpted from E. Regenstein, M. Connors, R. Romero-Jurado, & J. Weiner, *Uses and Misuses of Kindergarten Readiness Assessment Results* (Policy Conversations No. 6, 2017), www.startearly.org/app/uploads/pdf/PolicyConversationKRA2017.pdf.

Cover Photo Credits

Library of Congress Control Number: 2023938155

ISBN: 978-1-952331-25-1

Item: 1168

Contents

Introduction

Hilary Seitz

A few giggling girls, a couple of chatting children, and one questioning kindergartner all greet me as I enter Jesse Perez's kindergarten and first grade classroom in Anchorage School District. It is the district-mandated literacy block time, and most of the 24 children are working on a phonological awareness activity using letters printed on small squares of paper to match beginning sounds with picture cards. Several small groups of children are seated at round tables. Some children are working independently, others in pairs or triads. As I walk by a table, two children jump up to show me their letter-picture matches. Another child asks me to sit next to her, shows me a picture of a thimble, and asks what it is. Around the room, I see and hear children reading, naming, and sounding out letters; identifying pictures out loud; holding pencils with a pincer grasp; smiling at and talking with each other; and making connections with the word or picture.

Each child appears to have a sense of agency and purpose and feel comfortable and safe in this environment.

Jesse sits with four children in a small circle on the carpet. She asks each child questions about the letter sounds and records their answers on a clipboard. Meanwhile, a teaching assistant walks around the tables, writing short comments on yellow Post-it notes.

In this vignette, both the teacher and the teaching assistant are observing and assessing multiple behaviors and skills during this literacy block. They document the children's learning with informal observations, such as who is working together or independently, and with assessments of specific skills associated with phonological learning. Some of the informal observations are intentional while others are chance observations of behaviors and skills.

During this brief experience, Jesse takes note of the following informal observations:

- **Child-initiated experiences,** or what a child chooses to engage in
- **Work preferences,** or which children prefer to work by themselves and which are more interested in a social interaction
- **Behaviors,** or how attentive and self-directed children are while engaging in tasks and how collaborative and supportive they are to other children
- **Abilities,** or which children need more challenging work and which need additional help
- **Ideas and interests,** or what children connect with

The teacher is also able to document formal observations and assess learning, such as

- A specific child's progress on a speech and language Individualized Education Program (IEP) goal
- Reading progress and abilities related to specific skills (e.g., sounds that letters are making, letters and sounds that go together in words) on a state-required literacy assessment
- Developmental screening tools that document milestones, such as motor skills needed to hold a pencil

The list could go on depending on what other information Jesse wishes to learn or record on any given day.

Intentionally listening to children, watching their actions and behaviors during authentic learning experiences, and then documenting those observations helps her learn about all of the children she teaches. Observations like these provide Jesse with evidence to guide curriculum, learning experiences, and teaching strategies that support her class as a whole as well as each and every child as an individual, including specific considerations for children who may have disabilities or special needs or who speak more than one language. Multiple observations help teachers understand all learners better.

In today's world of data collection, high-stakes testing, and accountability, it is vitally important to understand effective ways to assess young children in familiar settings and to communicate this information with staff, families, and communities (Moses 2023). There are varying assessment strategies and tools for different age groups. For an infant, a teacher may use a formal checklist of developmental areas; for a 3-year-old, a teacher may take photos to accompany their noted observations of development; for a kindergartner, a teacher may oversee a kindergarten readiness state assessment.

Applying a variety of observation, documentation, and authentic assessment tools and methods with children supports a developmentally appropriate curriculum and helps to tell the whole story of a child's abilities through a strengths-based approach (NAEYC 2020).

Carrying on the work of *Spotlight on Young Children: Observation and Assessment* (Bohart & Procopio 2018), this book explores how to use observation, documentation, and assessment in early learning settings that serve children from birth through age 8, featuring current research and context on these essential topics. This collection of articles from NAEYC's *Young Children* journal and *Teaching Young Children* magazine provides readers with fundamental ideas and practical strategies to observe and assess children in their authentic learning environments using informal and formal assessments with intentionality.

This volume highlights aspects of observation and assessment in three distinct parts.

Part One: Purposes of Observation and Assessment showcases a variety of reasons why educators use observation and assessment, with information about the foundations and meanings behind them. These articles address how educators learn to see children's thinking, learning, development, and engagement.

Part Two: Strategies for Observing and Assessing provides methods that highlight different facets of the authentic assessment process and how to capture thinking and learning moments.

Part Three: Assessment Practices to Support Inclusion addresses reflecting on, celebrating, and including all children. These articles feature information on identifying children's unique strengths and needs, observing classrooms, and using a variety of strategies that support all children.

Each article is accompanied by reflection questions to connect and apply the ideas to your own teaching context. The entire collection demonstrates the critical roles observation and assessment play in the early learning setting. This extensive information and the authors' innovative strategies will guide you to better see and address how each and every child you work with is learning.

REFERENCES

Bohart, H., & R. Procopio 2018. *Spotlight on Young Children: Observation and Assessment.* Washington, DC: NAEYC.

Moses, A. 2023. "Developmentally Appropriate Assessment Practices: Gathering, Understanding, and Using Information." *Young Children* 78 (1): 4–5.

NAEYC. 2020. "Developmentally Appropriate Practice." Position statement. Washington, DC: NAEYC. www.naeyc.org/resources/position-statements/dap.

About the Editor

Hilary Seitz, PhD, is director for educator and leadership programs in the California State University system. She advocates and supports statewide efforts to support early childhood education and the new California PK–3 Early Childhood Education Specialist Instruction Credential. Dr. Seitz is professor emerita in early childhood education at the University of Alaska Anchorage. Her research areas have been in early literacy development, collaborative practices between families and schools including culturally responsive pedagogies, emergent curriculum development, documentation, authentic assessment, and social constructivist learning theories inspired by Reggio Emilia practices.

Purposes of Observation and Assessment

PART ONE

"Observing, documenting, and assessing each child's development and learning are essential processes for educators and programs to plan, implement, and evaluate the effectiveness of the experiences they provide to children" (NAEYC 2020, 19). To use observation and assessment effectively with young children, you must first understand the purposes and foundations of observation and assessment. Teachers, administrators, and families need to consider what assessment is and how it can be used in the early learning setting with different age groups (e.g., infants, toddlers, preschoolers, kindergartners, primary grade children). Documentation provides the stories and evidence of learning and helps to make learning visible.

The three articles in this part share insights into various purposes of observation and assessment, laying the foundation for a comprehensive system of observation, assessment, and documentation.

To begin, **Catherine Scott-Little,** with **Kathy L. Reschke,** defines assessment, introduces key concepts, and provides concrete steps about how to use authentic assessment in your classroom in "Foundations of Assessment for Preschool Settings."

"Meaningful Assessment and Documentation: How Directors Can Support Teaching and Learning," by **Debbie LeeKeenan** and **Iris Chin Ponte,** helps readers understand the responsibilities that directors have when overseeing programs and guiding teachers. This article presents an overview of the various aspects of assessment and includes many examples.

Natacha Ndabahagamye Jones, Amber T. Fowler, and **Jennifer Keys Adair** authored the third article, "Assessing Agency in Learning Contexts: A First, Critical Step to Assessing Children." In it, they describe ways to look for and document learning in children, with a particular emphasis on the value of children's agency.

REFERENCE

NAEYC. 2020. "Developmentally Appropriate Practice." Position statement. Washington, DC: NAEYC. www.naeyc.org/resources/position-statements/dap.

Foundations of Assessment for Preschool Settings

Catherine Scott-Little, with Kathy L. Reschke

Four-year-old Bre is quite verbal and expresses her ideas with a lot of confidence, but her teacher, Ms. Dhawan, has concerns about Bre's early math skills. For example, Bre says number words but not in the correct order ("One, four, six"). According to the state early learning standards, by the end of preschool, children should demonstrate one-to-one correspondence to 20, name the number of objects in a set of five, and recognize and sort basic shapes. Ms. Dhawan has noticed that Bre has room for growth in each of these mathematics skills.

Ms. Dhawan enriches Bre's day with a feast of mathematics learning opportunities focused on her interests indoors and outside. For example, during outdoor time, the teacher observes that Bre sorts and even makes a pattern with leaves. Inside, the teacher adds materials to create a family area restaurant, which offers Bre and her peers many opportunities to count and incorporate mathematical thinking. Ms. Dhawan also asks Bre's grandmother about Bre's interests and strengths at home. They talk about how Bre loves to accompany her grandmother to the grocery store and about opportunities to strengthen Bre's understanding of math while shopping.

Ms. Dhawan's observations and review of assessment data help her recognize that Bre needs more intentionally planned math experiences, starting with her interests and what she already knows and can do. Ms. Dhawan regularly observes and documents Bre's work and challenges her as she gains new skills. Along the way, she uses the state's standards to understand how mathematical skills develop and to expand and individualize her teaching. By the end of the year, Bre meets and exceeds all of the indicators for preschool children.

Contributed by Amanda Bryans

As shown in the opening vignette, preschool educators have many things to consider and do when it comes to assessment. In this article, we define assessment and offer important considerations for assessment in early childhood education. This article is an excerpt from our chapter in *Developmentally Appropriate Practice in Early Childhood Programs Serving Children from Birth Through Age 8*, Fourth Edition. More extensive examples and guidelines can be found in the chapter.

What Is Assessment?

Assessment is a systematic means of collecting and documenting information about children's learning and development to monitor children's progress toward learning goals, make curriculum decisions, and improve teaching practices. Early childhood educators use the assessment process to gather information about what children know and are able to do in order to understand their development and support their progress toward learning goals. They use this information to make informed decisions about teaching and about services for children. The process involves three steps.

- **Step 1**: Gathering information about children's learning and development is done through a variety of means. Educators observe children throughout the day, talk with them, and carefully consider what children are doing and saying. These informal observations play a key role in understanding children's learning and progress toward developmental and educational goals. Educators also learn about children by using assessment tools, which are specific measures used to collect information about children. (See "Authentic and Meaningful Developmental Screening in Early Childhood" on page 110 for more.)

- **Step 2**: Documentation is the important step of recording what is observed or learned through the assessment process. Documentation can be done by writing down observations (through anecdotal notes or other means), recording children's answers/responses to specific tasks on forms, filling out checklists, taking pictures or videos of children's accomplishments, or other means of capturing information about children.
- **Step 3**: Reflection is the process of looking at the information that has been documented, thinking about what it means about the child, and making decisions about learning experiences and interactions that would best support the child's development. Reflection can take place individually or with coteachers and family members and, depending on the situation, with the children who are being assessed.

Each of these steps is necessary for teachers to understand, make decisions about, and support children's learning and development. Because each of these three steps is essential to the process, we use the term *assessment* to refer to this full three-step process. Although assessment is a step-by-step process, it's also a process that is ongoing—to effectively assess children's growth and development, the steps are repeated over time to build understanding of the child's progress.

Assessment Methods in Early Childhood Education

Educators, like Ms. Dhawan in the opening vignette, draw on a variety of developmentally appropriate assessment methods to gain a fuller picture of a child's development and learning. Assessment methods range from anecdotal or unplanned opportunities, where an educator observes what a child says and does during daily activities, to formal procedures that must be carried out the same way with each child. Anecdotal observations that educators make naturally as part of daily routines and learning experiences are an important source of information to inform the assessment process and to better understand children's interests, knowledge, and skills. Sometimes these observations are spontaneous, such as when a child asks a question or does something that an educator happens to notice. For instance, an educator might observe that a preschooler uses a new word during lunchtime. Other times educators may plan specific activities to give children a real-world task where they can demonstrate their knowledge or skills. For example, an educator might ask a child to count out a certain number of crayons to see if they are able to count and group objects.

Educators also use assessment tools to help them gather and document information about children, and these tools generally fall into one of two broad categories or types.

- **Informal assessment tools:** This type of assessment tool enables educators to collect information about children's knowledge and development using a specified process but with latitude about how the assessment process is carried out. They are systematic but do not have to be done in exactly the same way with each child, and they may include observations of children during routine activities or as they participate in designated activities designed to document learning. Examples include ratings an educator fills out based on observations of a child, checklists that families fill out to rate a child's skills or behaviors, and portfolios that include samples of a child's drawing or writing. Because informal assessment is ongoing, the results give educators information about where children are in their skill development and can be used to show how they have progressed over time.

- **Formal assessment tools:** Formal assessment tools are used to measure what children have learned at a specific point in time and have specified procedures for how to collect the information. The process is carried out in a prescribed manner to ensure that every child is assessed the same way and that the results are evaluated or scored the same way for all children. In doing so, educators can compare an individual child's performance with other children. Tools that are used to screen children for potential disabilities are examples of formal assessments.

No matter the method or what is being assessed, assessment should always be authentic—that is, by using age-appropriate approaches, tools and methods that are culturally relevant, and a language the child understands.

Considerations Regarding the Assessment Process

There are important considerations regarding the assessment process and assessment tools as they are used with all children, including why an assessment is being used, the age of the child involved, and the need for varied and multiple assessments.

1. **The purpose for which the assessment process is being conducted.** Effective assessment processes begin with a careful examination of the purpose of the process, followed by informed decisions about what assessment strategy or tools to use based on the purpose. For example, if you feel that a child might have a language delay, you might use a screening that assesses the number of words the child knows to determine if the child's language development should be evaluated formally. If the purpose is to monitor children's progress and develop individualized lesson plans, then informal formative assessment tools based on the learning goals for specific children are most appropriate.
2. **The age of the child.** Assessment measures, particularly formal assessment tools, are usually developed for a specified age range or grade level. Therefore, the assessment tool must fit the age of the children being assessed. Anecdotal observations and informal formative assessments designed by teachers are effective with all ages to collect information on children's development and learning, but formal assessment tools should be used with children who are within the designated age range for which the tool is designed.

3. **The different ways children may demonstrate their skills and knowledge.** Educators use multiple assessment strategies to get a complete picture of what children know and are able to do. The use of multiple assessment strategies gives children the best opportunity to demonstrate their competencies because one type of assessment tool may not adequately reflect a child's competencies.

Assessment with Diverse Groups

Educators typically have children with a range of backgrounds and abilities in their classrooms. It is essential to take intentional steps to make sure that all children are assessed fairly and in the way that best suits the child. A critical step in the process is for educators to reflect on and work against biases that may get in the way of assessing a child accurately and using the results from the assessment appropriately.

Steps to minimize the impact biases can have on the assessment process include the following:

- Recognizing how one's own culture can affect expectations for children, the way children are assessed, and the judgments made based on assessment results.
- Focusing on documenting children's strengths rather than looking for ways they may demonstrate deficits or not meet expectations.
- Using multiple assessment strategies, including anecdotal observations and informal assessment tools so that children have multiple ways to demonstrate their competencies. Doing so can help educators take into account cultural differences, with the understanding that not all children demonstrate what they have learned in the same way.

- Paying careful attention to whether the assessment tool has been shown to be reliable and valid for use with children who have similar characteristics to the children being assessed and, if not, being very cautious when interpreting and using the results. This includes taking children's linguistic backgrounds into account in how the assessment is carried out (what language is used) and who is involved (an interpreter, insights from families). Educators can also advocate for more appropriate practices if assessment tools are not a good fit for the children they are assessing.

About the Authors

Catherine Scott-Little, PhD, is professor of human development and family studies at University of North Carolina at Greensboro, where she codirects and teaches in the birth through kindergarten graduate program. Her areas of expertise include state-level policies, such as early learning and development standards, assessment systems, and teacher education.

Kathy L. Reschke, PhD, is an early childhood education consultant specializing in the development and learning of children birth through age 5 and the interactions and environments that best support them. She is experienced in and passionate about creating engaging, valued resources and learning experiences for early childhood educators, particularly in online spaces.

Reflection Questions

1. What informal and formal assessment tools do you use in your early learning program? Why do you use these tools?
2. Describe the steps you use to assess children in your program. How do you gather information? How do you document the information you collect? How do you reflect on the information you learn?
3. How do the assessment strategies you use help you learn about the individual cultures and strengths of each child in your program?
4. What resources and supports would help you incorporate appropriate assessment practices in your daily work with children?

Photographs: p. 6, © NAEYC; pp. 9, 10, © Getty Images

This article is excerpted and adapted from C. Scott-Little with K.L. Reschke, "Observing, Documenting, and Assessing Children's Development and Learning," in *Developmentally Appropriate Practice in Early Childhood Programs Serving Children from Birth Through Age 8*, 4th ed., NAEYC (Washington, DC: NAEYC, 2022), 159–80.

Meaningful Assessment and Documentation

How Directors Can Support Teaching and Learning

Debbie LeeKeenan and Iris Chin Ponte

Pay attention.

Be astonished.

Tell about it.

—Mary Oliver, *Red Bird*

Directors have a diverse set of responsibilities, and managing them all can often feel like a delicate balancing act. You have to provide a safe, healthy environment for children and teachers. Hire and retain a qualified, diverse staff. Have a solid business plan. Understand child development and best practices in early childhood education. Establish collaborative relationships with families and program stakeholders. Market your program. Help out in a classroom when you're needed. Take time to care for your own physical and emotional health. Remain calm under pressure.

Your overall responsibility is to create a physically and emotionally safe educational environment where learning and care can flourish for children, staff, and families. To do this, you must prioritize your duties and tasks on an ongoing basis and focus on what is most important at any particular moment, even as you keep an eye on the long term. And to do that, you need to embrace observation and assessment as basic tools of your director's toolbox.

Through observation and assessment, you collect data that provide evidence of what is working or not working in your program and in the classroom. Using this information, you and the teachers can make informed decisions on improvement plans and goal setting. While there are various types of assessments (ranging from safety checklists to community surveys), this article explores methods for demonstrating what children are learning and the many benefits of thoughtful documentation.

What Are Children Learning?

When you walk into a classroom, you notice the physical environment—how the room is arranged, what's on the walls, what materials and books are displayed and how. You see how children are interacting with each other and how the teacher is interacting with them. While these observations can often give you an idea of the program's quality, this is not enough.

Assessment of children's work and growth is critical for directors and teachers to consider. While it is the teachers' responsibility to focus on individual children, you need to keep the big picture in mind and develop an assessment plan that connects with your program's values, goals, and curriculum approach. The assessment plan should answer the questions "How do children show what they know?" and "How can we best determine what children are learning and what they are ready to learn next?"

Some programs choose standard assessment tools, such as COR Advantage and The Work Sampling System, to use with children at certain checkpoints throughout the year. Such assessment tools are commonly linked to specific curriculum models; for example, COR Advantage is linked to the HighScope Curriculum, and the assessment program Teaching Strategies GOLD is linked to The Creative Curriculum. These assessments can be time consuming, but they are useful in maintaining consistency across the center. They also provide a helpful framework for teachers who are less experienced with child development and assessment, easing the director's burden in developing a system that works for everyone.

Other programs create an assessment portfolio for each child. These portfolios can include

- Children's work samples from throughout the year
- Teachers' observation notes
- Photos of children's work
- Children's reflections on their work

In some cases, the portfolio moves with the child to the next year of their education. In order for the portfolio to serve as a comprehensive record of a child's learning and development, teachers should also take the time to label children's work and document the child's thoughts and comments about their own work. In other words, a portfolio is not just a collection of work but a very intentionally curated compilation that clearly demonstrates certain aspects of a child's developmental growth and progress.

Portfolios also offer an opportunity to help children reflect on their own learning. A teacher might ask a child to review some of their work samples and think about which ones they are most proud of and why, or what they learned while doing the activity or work. Teachers also ask children to select some of the items to include in their portfolios.

Assessment Methods

Methods for assessing what children know and can do fall on a continuum from formal to informal (Epstein et al. 2004). On one end are standardized tests that are *norm referenced*—meaning "a child's performance is interpreted by comparing it to the performance of a group of peers, or *norming group*, who have previously taken the same test" (Bodrova & Leong 2018, 18). Such tests are often used to obtain and report information about children's development for the purpose of program evaluation and funding. Norm-referenced screening instruments may be used to identify potential sensory, cognitive, or social and emotional challenges as part of a child's ongoing assessment in a program. A formal evaluation is often initiated when a child's teacher or family has questions about the child's development and wants to identify potential delays or disabilities and make a referral for specialized services.

Authentic assessment appears on the more informal end of the assessment continuum. It is the ongoing process of gathering evidence about children's learning, development, performance, and understanding that is used to guide planning and instruction (Bagnato, Neisworth, & Pretti-Frontczak 2010). It involves observing and documenting children's learning in the context of their daily activities and routines. The table on page 15 identifies the various components of authentic assessment. This information is important for both directors and teachers to understand. While teachers are directly implementing these practices with children, you need to make intentional decisions to support them in using these approaches appropriately and effectively.

What Is Documentation?

Documentation is the process of systematically "observing, recording, interpreting, and sharing" evidence of children's learning (Krechevsky et al. 2013, 59). Teachers document children's work in a number of ways, including collecting drawing and writing samples, taking photographs of a structure made outdoors with natural materials, noting observations of a child's processes and interactions making audio or video recordings of dramatic play scenarios, and transcribing a child's thoughts and questions about their own work.

To be useful, documentation must be intentional and planned. Effective documentation makes children's learning visible in ways that help inform educators', families', and policymakers' understanding of and reflection on children's development and thinking processes. While documenting children's learning is primarily a responsibility of teachers, your leadership and support of them in this process are critical to its usefulness.

Components of Authentic Assessment

Components	Some Questions to Focus On	Tools
Monitor Keep track of the child's learning experiences.	› What projects have they participated in? › What materials did they use? › How do they approach learning?	› Checklists › Inventories › Class lists › Journal entries
Observe Gather information about the child by watching and listening.	› Note general impressions of the child. › How do they interact with others? › Are they engaged with the activity?	› Systematic observations › Anecdotal records › Running records (noting all behaviors a child exhibits to help determine their thinking process) › Audio and video recordings › Photographs
Interact Find out what the child knows, feels, believes, and understands.	› Ask clarifying and probing questions to better understand the child's thinking. › Challenge the child's current thinking and help them move beyond where they are.	› Questioning techniques (Why do you think . . . ? What if . . . ? Tell me more about . . . I wonder . . .) › Interviews › Checklists › Response journals
Analyze Gather and review artifacts of the child's learning; seek the family's input.	› What evidence do you have to demonstrate the child's learning and progress? › When examining artifacts, consider both content and process. › What does the child's family see them doing at home and in the community?	› Written or dictated stories and reports › Writing and drawing samples › Audio and video recordings › Portfolios › Photographs › Rubrics › Family surveys › Conversations with the family at home or in the center
Report Organize the data in a meaningful way and share it with the family, director, and others.	› Involve the child in this process by asking questions (Which drawing of your block construction would you like me to put in your portfolio? Why this one? Tell me more about this drawing).	› Family conferences › Progress reports › Narratives about the child written by the teacher › Self-assessment › Portfolios › Rubrics
Link to instruction Use the data to inform instruction and practice.	› Ask questions to improve individualized teaching strategies (How can I use the child's interest in robots to engage them during circle time? Would this child be more likely to spend longer periods of time in the language arts center if I included more books about foxes?).	› All of the above

Beyond recording and evaluating children's work, documentation has many benefits. It serves as a way to revisit experiences and extend thinking for children. It helps teachers plan curriculum because it links observation, planning, implementation, and assessment. For program leaders, it's also a way to communicate and share what is going on in the center and the classroom with others (children, families, teachers, and the community). Documentation can bring people together in a diverse community, celebrate similarities and differences, and create a shared history.

Families especially appreciate seeing tangible evidence of their children's learning processes, as in the following vignette:

> Marisol is a 5-year-old in Penelope's preschool class at Sandy Shore Playgroup. At pickup time one afternoon, Marisol's grandfather, Oscar, remarks to the program director, Isla, that he doesn't think Marisol is "really learning anything" and that he is worried that she won't be ready for kindergarten. Isla suggests that the two of them and Penelope meet to discuss his concerns. Before the meeting, Isla and Penelope discuss how to best explain the program's curriculum to Marisol's grandfather. As part of this preparation, they also review the portfolio and documentation Penelope has compiled about Marisol over the last few months and select pieces to share with her family.
>
> At the meeting, they give Oscar an overview of the program's curriculum approach and how it connects to the program's learning goals and to state standards. What really seems to convince him of Marisol's progress and put him at ease are the samples of documentation they show him. There is a short story partly written and partly dictated by Marisol about her thoughts on one of her favorite books, *Strega Nona,* by Tomie dePaola, as well as photos showing her creating her own art based on the book's illustrations. Finally, there is an anecdotal narrative written by Penelope about her observation that Marisol understood the story plot and was able to express her thoughts orally and in writing (language and literacy skills). Penelope also noted Marisol's attention to detail as she carefully mimicked the original artwork in her own drawing (creative expression and fine motor skills).
>
> Oscar beams with pride for his granddaughter as he pores over these materials, even seeming a little surprised at the complexity of thought Marisol's work shows. At the end of the meeting, he tells Isla and Penelope that he looks forward to seeing more documentation during the year.

Moving Toward a Culture of Documentation

If the teachers in your program do not already document children's work, they might be resistant or feel it is just one more thing they need to work into an already full routine. It's your responsibility to discuss the merits of the practice and listen to teachers' input in order to collectively adopt and establish a culture of documentation. The following will help you support and collaborate with the teachers in this process:

- **Create an atmosphere where teachers feel comfortable exploring and experimenting with different methods of documentation to figure out what works best for them.** For example, with your encouragement, a teacher might try recording a video and taking photos before they discover that writing a learning story—a short, narrative story about what they observed—about the small group of children taking apart an old, broken toy to see how it works is the approach that best helps them reflect on the children's interests and how they can extend their learning.
- **Provide the necessary tools, time, and support.** To make documentation an integral part of the program, teachers need convenient access to tools (e.g., computers, digital cameras, printers, display boards). Documentation takes time, practice, and focus. If you ask teachers to create individual portfolios and high-quality documentation, they need dedicated time to do this work.
- **Offer direction and structure to the process, as needed.** Some teachers may feel overwhelmed with the documentation process or unsure of where to start. Provide samples or templates for documentation displays, portfolios, and newsletters.

Whether you're introducing documentation to your program or simply trying to improve its effectiveness, ask teachers to consider what they are documenting and why. The subject and goal should be identified first, and then the documentation format can be considered—perhaps it works better as an entry in the child's journal rather than a wall display. Determine if the documentation will simply be descriptive or also include an analysis of what's being observed. Encourage teachers to consider how the documentation can be interactive and invite feedback. Will children review the documentation and share their thoughts on what happened? How might families share their feedback?

Practical Tips for Facilitating Documentation

- Establish documentation policies and procedures that cover confidentiality and uploading, handling, and sharing photographs and other files securely.
- If you expect teachers to use technology, such as recording devices and editing software, provide them with appropriate training.
- Facilitate use of the center's common areas and other shared spaces outside of individual classrooms (e.g., hallways, reception areas, the staff lunchroom) for teachers to take turns using as strategic locations to display documentation.
- Technology can sometimes make it too easy to indiscriminately take a lot of photos or record reams of dialogue and lose sight of what is important. Emphasize quality over quantity. Remind teachers to pause before snapping a photograph and ask themselves some questions: What is a good photo? What kind of documentation is meaningful? Who is the documentation for? How can we use our materials with care?

- Documentation does not need to be a time-consuming venture. Just taking time to reflect on practice and experiences in the classroom is valuable. For example, at one center, classroom teachers took turns at each staff meeting bringing a piece of student work, such as a child's drawing, to have a group discussion about it. If teachers need some prompting, ask questions like "What do you notice in the drawing?," "What do you think the child was thinking about?," and "What are your next steps?"

One director explained the process she used to include documentation in her program:

> After we made the schoolwide decision to make documentation a collective focus, we had many workshops and discussions about documentation at our monthly staff meetings, head teacher meetings, and retreats. It became a professional development priority. I realized it was important to create an environment that allowed people to take risks, try new ideas, make mistakes, and try again. Teachers were given permission to mess around and do different things. We gave every class a digital camera. It was only then that we realized there are no-, low-, and high-tech documentation methods, and there are benefits to each. There is documentation that is beautifully mounted and planned, and there is quick and dirty documentation—the end-of-the-day message written on newsprint or on a white board. All kinds of documentation have value.

You can use documentation to invite input from all constituencies. Provide sticky notes and a pencil next to a documentation panel so viewers can note their reactions and questions about the documentation. For example, you might give children the opportunity to create self-portraits and answer prompts asking them to describe themselves, such as their interests ("I like ________") or something more open ended they choose to share ("One thing you should know about me is ________"). Together, the self-portraits and self-descriptions can be assembled into a documentation display that celebrates differences and individuality, inspires self-esteem, and encourages conversation and excitement—both in the center hallways and in the wider program community.

While documentation requires you to invest time and resources, the benefits show the practice's worth. It serves as an equal exchange among all members of the school community and is the representation of a loving community that cares for children, families, and teachers alike.

Conclusion

Using a variety of methods to assess children's learning is a vital part of measuring your program's effectiveness, ensuring its continued advancement toward the mission and goals you've set, and supporting children's development. Work closely with constituents—including teachers and families—to understand the different types of assessment to help you identify the right ones for your program.

It is best practice to make sure families have reviewed the program's assessment plan and have an opportunity to raise concerns about any part of it. Remember that "high-stakes decisions about a child" should never be based on just one formal evaluation (Riley-Ayers 2018, 2). A comprehensive, holistic view of the child—including, when appropriate, culturally and linguistically appropriate standardized assessment tools—should be used. Documentation can be used to communicate the children's learning and development with families and others in a visually based, engaging way.

REFERENCES

Bagnato, S.J., J.T. Neisworth, & K. Pretti-Frontczak. 2010. *LINKing Authentic Assessment and Early Childhood Intervention: Best Measures for Best Practices.* 2nd ed. Baltimore: Brookes.

Bodrova, E., & D.J. Leong. 2018. "Common Assessment Terms and How to Use Them: A Glossary for Early Childhood Educators." In *Spotlight on Young Children: Observation and Assessment,* eds. H. Bohart & R. Procopio, 15–20. Washington, DC: NAEYC.

Epstein, A.S., L.J. Schweinhart, A. DeBruin-Parecki, & K.B. Robin. 2004. "Preschool Assessment: A Guide to Developing a Balanced Approach." *Preschool Policy Matters,* Issue 7. New Brunswick, NJ: National Institute for Early Education Research (NIEER); Ypsilanti, MI: HighScope Educational Research Foundation. http://nieer.org/wp-content/uploads/2016/08/7-1.pdf.

Krechevsky, M., B. Mardell, M. Rivard, & D. Wilson. 2013. *Visible Learners: Promoting Reggio-Inspired Approaches in All Schools.* San Francisco: Jossey-Bass.

Riley-Ayers, S. 2018. "Introduction." In *Spotlight on Young Children: Observation and Assessment,* eds. H. Bohart & R. Procopio, 1–5. Washington, DC: NAEYC.

Reflection Questions

1. Think about the system for data collection that your early learning program uses. Is it connected to your curriculum (such as how GOLD is linked to Creative Curriculum) or is your assessment system separate? If it is connected, does it provide information that is useful for you and children's families? If it is a separate system, such as a portfolio, how does it support the everyday activities in the classroom and connect to the state or program standards?
2. How do you share assessment information with families? What types of communication systems do you use? Do families have opportunities to ask questions?
3. If you are using authentic assessment strategies in your classroom or program, how do you collaborate with families in gathering data and sharing documentation?
4. Does your program provide resources, training, and/or time to make documentation an integral part of the program? What other types of supports could your program provide to help teachers be more successful?

About the Authors

Debbie LeeKeenan is an early childhood consultant, lecturer, and author. She was director and lecturer at the Eliot-Pearson Children's School, the laboratory school affiliated with the Eliot-Pearson Department of Child Study and Human Development at Tufts University, and is coauthor of *Leading Anti-Bias Early Childhood Programs: A Guide to Change, for Change,* Second Edition (Teachers College Press, 2023).

Iris Chin Ponte, PhD, is director and classroom teacher at the Henry Frost Children's Program in Belmont, MA. She also currently serves as an adjunct faculty member at Lesley University's Graduate School of Education. Iris previously worked for Sesame Street Research at the Children's Television Workshop (now Sesame Workshop).

Photographs: p. 12, © Getty Images; p. 16, courtesy of the authors

This article is excerpted and adapted from D. LeeKeenan and I.C. Ponte, *From Survive to Thrive: A Director's Guide for Leading an Early Childhood Program* (Washington, DC: NAEYC, 2018).

Assessing Agency in Learning Contexts

A First, Critical Step to Assessing Children

Natacha Ndabahagamye Jones, Amber T. Fowler, and Jennifer Keys Adair

It's center time, or "work time" as they call it in Ms. Amaya's and Ms. Jackson's pre-K inclusion classroom. A group of children are engaged with various materials and activities on one of the classroom rugs: Omar is putting together an airplane puzzle. Beto is building an aircraft with bristle blocks. Michael is alternating between reading a book aloud and playing.

Ms. Jackson is sitting on the rug, holding up *The Duckling Gets a Cookie!?* by Mo Willems for Michael to read.

Michael: (*Reads the mischievous pigeon's line loudly and dramatically.*) "Noooooooooooo!"

Ms. Jackson: That's a long no, right Michael?

Beto pauses his play to look at the book and listens as Michael continues his animated reading.

Michael: (*Reads in mock frustration.*) "It's not fair!"

Omar turns around to look at Michael, then looks at the book and laughs. Ms. Jackson laughs too as she turns the page. Beto smiles. As he continues to build, he starts adding dialogue to his play with the aircraft.

Beto: Hello? Knock, knock!

Michael: (*Props himself on his knees and reads as his body sways.*) "Pigeons like cookies too! WHY DID YOU GET THAT COOKIE?"

Michael's faked exasperation is met with more laughter.

In this pre-K inclusion classroom in the southern United States, teachers are intentional about setting up the learning context—or the space, schedule, and expectations—to encourage children to initiate and influence engagements in their environment. Teachers "create and foster a community of learners" (NAEYC 2020, 15) in which children can build on skills, abilities, or competence by following their interests and ideas. During work time, children use their agency to interact with materials and each other in open-ended, child-directed ways. This allows teachers to observe and document their capabilities and skills authentically.

For Michael, a 4-year-old Black boy with autism spectrum disorder (ASD), this context fostered his joyful learning and created opportunities for him to achieve his full potential (NAEYC 2020). Michael enacted his agency to read, express, and share something that he enjoys. He got to choose a book and take the lead in reading it from a spot that was physically comfortable and where he could move his body. His experience reading to his teacher and classmates both demonstrated and expanded a range of academic and social and emotional knowledge, skills, and talents. This allowed Ms. Jackson to encourage Michael with verbal and nonverbal feedback and to observe that

- He is an avid reader with a reading level and abilities that exceed grade-level expectations.
- He is expanding his ability to lift words from the page in a way that is engaging and exciting for him and his community.
- He explores the range of his voice, refines his reading abilities, and shares what he reads with peers who are playing around him.
- He experiences the joy of contributing to his classmates' laughter and enjoyment.

In Michael's classroom, he was able to exercise his agency regularly, with the knowledge that it would be welcomed instead of disciplined (Park et al. 2021). Yet in rigid, overly structured early learning environments that prioritize compliance and control, young children cannot show what they know and can do (Adair & Colegrove 2021). This is particularly true in state-funded programs that serve communities of color that are economically challenged (Early et al. 2010). In this article, we explain the need to assess learning environments to determine whether young children have the agency to demonstrate their full range of abilities, interests, and knowledge. We then lay out how educators can use these environments in their assessment practices. The examples described and documented are drawn from two multisite, large-scale studies: *Agency and Young Children* (Adair 2014; Adair & Colegrove 2021) and *Civic Action and Young Children* (McManus et al. 2019; Payne et al. 2020). These studies focus on the range of capabilities and communal and civic engagements young children of color demonstrate when they are provided ample amounts of agency in their daily schooling contexts.

Agency and Young Children

The *Agency and Young Children Study* was funded by the Foundation for Child Development and recently published as a book titled *Segregation by Experience: Agency, Racism and Learning in the Early Grades.* In this study, researchers spent one academic year in a first-grade classroom where children of Latino/a/x immigrants and African American children had an atypical amount of agency—or choices, freedom, time, and space to follow their interests and ideas. Children demonstrated a significant range of capability expansion that is hard or impossible to see in controlling, strict classrooms.

Now, in a study funded by the Brady Education Foundation, researchers are testing a culturally flexible tool that will support agency in classrooms so that more children—particularly children of color—will be offered dynamic and sophisticated learning experiences that support their agency and capability expansion. You can learn more about this work at http://sites.edb.utexas.edu/agency-and-young-children.

Agency Supports Sophisticated Learning and Community Building

We (the authors) share identities and experiences as early childhood researchers, teacher educators, former early childhood teachers, and mothers. We also share the belief that children are smart, capable, and caring. They deserve to receive dynamic, sophisticated, community-rooted, and culturally sustaining learning experiences in their everyday schooling. We approach learning as an active endeavor in which teachers support young children's agency to move, observe, initiate, and engage to see themselves as capable and competent.

Our backgrounds bring a range of perspectives. Natacha Ndabahagamye Jones (first author) is a Black immigrant woman, a doctoral candidate, and a past research participant in the *Agency and Young Children Study* led by Jennifer Keys Adair (third author). Amber T. Fowler (second author) is a Black woman born in the United States and a doctoral student. She experienced her childhood as a foster child in the southern United States. Jennifer Keys Adair is a White woman born in the United States, a professor, and a researcher who has studied agency with BIPOC (Black and Indigenous people of color) communities for 15 years.

Assessing young children authentically requires educators to understand the various and complex ways children make meaning through the reciprocal relationships they have with adults, their learning environments, and multiple communities (Carr & Lee 2012; Darling-Hammond & Snyder 2000; NAEYC 2020). We take the position that teachers, administrators, and other educational stakeholders must assess, or evaluate, these learning contexts before requiring young children to be directly assessed. Doing so ensures that

- Children are provided multiple and consistent opportunities to use their agency.
- Children are able to show the full range of their capabilities.
- Educators select and use strengths-based assessments that recognize and support children's capabilities and the holistic ways they learn, including through play.

Along with our colleagues in the Agency and Young Children Research Collective, we have studied how agency impacts the learning and development of young children from African American and Latino/a/x immigrant and nonimmigrant communities (Adair 2014; Adair & Colegrove 2021). Our research and practice have shown that when young children have multiple and consistent opportunities to use their agency, they develop, demonstrate, and refine sophisticated knowledge-making skills that are essential to their learning and growth. These skills and ways of knowing include observation, inquiry, open-ended discussion, critical and creative thinking, problem solving, and initiative (Gopnik 2012; Helm & Katz 2016; NAEYC 2020; Souto-Manning et al. 2019). They are critical to child development and equitable learning.

Consistent access to agentic learning contexts fosters children's ability to expand on their curiosity and their cultural, linguistic, and embodied experiences. It also enhances their knowledge, skills, and sustained learning engagements. Agency facilitates young children's cocreation of caring and dynamic communities of learners, which provides many opportunities to show care; advocate for one another; negotiate and regulate their play, interactions, and access to resources; and balance individual needs with those of the community (Payne, Falkner, & Adair 2020). With agency, children demonstrate ownership of their learning and responsibility for each other's well-being and for an environment that reflects and honors multiple ways of being and learning.

Assessment Practices and Inequitable Access to Agentic Learning

While many educators and families would agree that agentic practices are desirable for young children, accountability pressures that prioritize academic skills, formal testing, individualized learning, and fewer opportunities for holistic and playful learning have become standard—even in early childhood education (Bassok, Latham, & Rorem 2016). Early childhood teachers are often expected to assess children in ways that are not developmentally, culturally, or linguistically responsive (Blessing 2019; Paris 2012). This significantly limits the attention they can give to creating caring, agentic, equitable learning contexts where children can fully demonstrate their knowledge and skills (Adair & Sachdeva 2021; Muller et al. 2022).

Many schooling contexts for young children of color prioritize controlling, measuring, and intervening rather than providing learning environments with multiple ways and opportunities for children to show what they know and can do (Cervantes-Soon, Degollado, & Nuñez 2020; Wright 2021). Denying young children their agency in school means they do not have much time to collaborate, problem solve, work through conflict, or experience other kinds of community- or civic-building activities. Most importantly, severely limiting agency also limits how many capabilities children can demonstrate. Imagine that Michael, from the opening vignette, was only allowed to read independently, sit still during specific times, engage with books chosen by his teacher, and be formally assessed out of context. He might not show the same skills and enthusiasm. His teachers would not be able to see the breadth of his skills, and he might not be able to expand on them.

To further illustrate, consider another instance from Ms. Amaya's and Ms. Jackson's pre-K inclusion classroom.

> One day at recess, Ms. Smith, a "floater teacher" who prioritizes control and compliance over agency and learning, is supervising the children's play. Michael is playing on a concrete accessibility ramp with a truck he brought over from the sand area. Ms. Smith tells him to keep the truck by the sand. Michael follows her instructions, but a minute later, he carries the truck to the ramp again. Ms. Smith scolds him and tells him to take the truck back. When he doesn't, she walks over and pulls Michael by the hand to the sand area. Moments later, Michael tries to move the truck again. Ms. Smith scolds him again.
>
> Ms. Amaya (the lead teacher) comes back from break and notices what Michael is doing. Ms. Smith leaves. Michael takes the truck back to the top of the ramp and pushes it down. He squeals with excitement and runs to get it. He goes back to the top, then pushes it again.
>
> Meanwhile, a group of girls are chasing each other on the ramp. One of them, Nicole, notices when the truck hits her feet and stops. Her feet have become a barrier. She moves her feet and opens them wide so that the truck can pass through. Michael runs to the bottom of the ramp, retrieves the truck, and runs back to the top. Nicole prepares for the truck to go through her legs again. She stands with her feet wide, trying to align them perfectly with Michael's truck. Michael pushes the truck, and it goes through Nicole's legs. Nicole starts moving all over the ramp so that Michael has to move and aim the truck to go through her legs. This experiment continues until Nicole runs off to the sand area. Ms. Amaya watches as Michael continues to push the truck down the ramp with children moving in and out of the scene.

During these interactions, Ms. Amaya observed that Michael demonstrated inquisitive and cognitive skills as he gained an emerging understanding of force, motion, gravity, friction, and velocity. However, she was most impressed by Michael's capabilities to include others in his play and to adapt what he was doing to the interests of those around him. Because he has ASD, Michael often played in isolated ways and struggled to include others. Pushing the truck down the ramp with Nicole demonstrated a range of expanded capabilities across many domains. Most importantly, Michael included others and contributed to a group endeavor.

If Ms. Smith had remained in charge, Michael's capabilities would not have been observed. This is not because he did not have them; rather, the learning context under Ms. Smith's direction did not allow Michael to show his full range of knowledge and interests. Likewise, if Ms. Smith had been the floater teacher when Michael started reading *The Duckling Gets a Cookie!?*, Michael might not have experienced the joy and contribution he did with Ms. Jackson. He might not have been able to demonstrate all of his skills, nor would his teachers have been able to observe them.

Assessing Contexts: Pushing Back Against Bias

Children are assessed in contexts assumed to be neutral; however, even well-intentioned adults may hold biases and assumptions about children's families, communities, and social identities (such as race, culture, languages, and abilities). Young children's "social identities bring with them socially constructed meanings that reflect biases targeted to marginalized groups, resulting in differential experiences of privilege and injustice" (NAEYC 2019, 14). In addition, the tools and methods used to assess young children can reinforce deficit views about children of color and their communities. This can occur even when the practices and materials used appear to be developmentally appropriate and/or culturally sustaining.

These deficit views are compounded by historical and ongoing individual and structural racism. Narratives of an "achievement gap" position children of color as deficient compared with White children and as problems to be "fixed" instead of a more accurate view: seeing the gap as an educational manifestation of social inequalities that are worsened by narrow, one-size-fits-all learning experiences (Boykin & Noguera 2011). Redressing these inequities refocuses our understanding of young children's knowledge making and curriculum as rooted in relationships and engaged participation. "Assessing a Learning Context for Agency" on this page offers some guidance on ensuring that learning contexts are caring, agentic, and equitable.

Assessing a Learning Context for Agency

Here are some questions we can ask ourselves as educators to assess whether our learning context supports children's agentic practices.

Do I/we

- ❑ Provide a range of opportunities for children to generate and share ideas?
- ❑ Listen to and follow up on children's ideas?
- ❑ Provide a range of opportunities for children to influence lessons, investigations, play, and other activities?
- ❑ Provide children multiple ways to demonstrate their knowledge?
- ❑ Allow children to share stories from their families and communities?
- ❑ Welcome children's full range of identities, interests, and languages?
- ❑ Offer multiple opportunities for children to work with each other?
- ❑ Provide multiple ways for children to contribute to and shape the classroom community?
- ❑ Observe and listen to children before intervening?
- ❑ Offer a range of opportunities to use space flexibly and move around often and in different ways?
- ❑ Support children using a variety of materials (natural or manmade) in a variety of ways?
- ❑ Give children time to explore what they are interested in within their environment (indoors and outdoors)?
- ❑ Encourage and welcome children's initiatives on how they advocate and care for one another and for their environment?

If we answer yes to any of these questions, we can also reflect on whether we make these experiences accessible to all children equitably or whether we make children earn or prove they are worthy of such experiences.

Agency Is a Requirement for Demonstrating Social and Collective Capabilities

It is transition time in Ms. Bailey's first-grade classroom. While she sets up for science, a group of children gather near the corner of the room where the class meets for mini lessons, read-alouds, and other whole group activities. Celeste and Robert are both sitting in their teacher's chair with the numbered craft sticks that Ms. Bailey uses for various activities. They are singing "Hickety Pickety Bumblebee" and disagree over the song's lyrics.

Celeste: It's hickety!

Robert: I said pickety! (*Continues singing "pickety pickety bumblebee."*)

Celeste: (*Smiles and models the proper lyrics patiently.*) Look. Hickety, pickety bumblebee.

They continue singing. Robert eventually gets up from the chair, and Celeste takes over the chant. She gains the attention of a few more classmates.

Celeste: Hickety, pickety bumblebee . . .

Diana: Who can sing their name for me?

Ms. Bailey pauses in her work and begins to watch the children. As she observes, Celeste shuffles through the craft sticks in search of Diana's number. Like most of the children, she has memorized her classmates' numbers and easily finds Diana's. Diana now sits in the teacher's chair with the craft sticks. She repeats the chant and calls on Kata, who is across the room. Kata comes immediately to sit in the teacher's chair.

Robert has moved over to face the alphabet chart and is using an apple-ended pointer to point to the letters. "This is *A*," he says, "and *A* says /a/. This is *B*, and *B* says /b/." Before Robert can get to letter *C*, Peter tries to pull the pointer from him but is unsuccessful. Peter holds his chest and smiles in defeat, then goes behind the easel to get a different pointer. Robert resumes the phoneme sounds.

Children learn best when they find relevance and connections to the learning and their environment (Souto-Manning 2014). Even in unplanned and transitional activities, children benefit when they have ample amounts of agency. They can "experience responsive interactions that nurture their full range of social, emotional, cognitive, physical, and linguistic abilities" (NAEYC 2019, 5), expand their multidimensional capabilities, and support the cocreation of a caring community of learners.

As seen in the vignette, the children in Ms. Bailey's class were able to move, explore, and be playful, even during transitions. The classroom tools they had access to also facilitated their learning and connections. As they engaged with one another and their environment, Ms. Bailey observed and documented a range of mathematical and early literacy skills and knowledge—some emerging, and some reaching mastery. For instance,

- Celeste and Robert demonstrated phonological awareness skills with the rhyming song.
- Robert demonstrated one-to-one correspondence, the ability to read left to right and sweep to the next line, letter recognition, and phonemic awareness as he tapped and said the name and sounds of each of the letters on the alphabet chart.
- Celeste could identify one- and two-digit numbers and match those numbers to the corresponding classmate's name.

Ms. Bailey was also able to observe and document communal, interpersonal, and social and emotional skills and engagements:

- Celeste and Robert were able to initiate an activity and share materials, including the teacher's chair.
- Celeste listened to her peer's chant and patiently corrected his error.
- Celeste knew which craft stick was Diana's. She sought it in the cup with an intent to call on her friend within the rules of the game they had established.
- Diana demonstrated an ability to expand a child-led activity to her class community when she chose Kata's craft stick.
- Kata's eagerness to join the game demonstrated she felt enjoyment and belonging as a community member.
- Robert and Peter figured out child-centered resolutions to seeking the same pointer. While some might conclude that the boys lacked self-regulation because they were fighting over the pointer, we see the opposite: the boys figured out a solution with no adult direction in order to return to the alphabet chart or move on to other activities.

Being a Keen Observer of Young Children

Often when we observe children, we watch them with the intent (conscious or not) to evaluate them. Keen observation is different. We are *keen observers* when we observe children's capabilities, interests, and relationships as well as where they spend time, what materials animate them, and what kinds of contributions they enjoy making to the classroom community. Replacing our evaluatory eyes with curious ones means we can focus on young children as human beings with interests, desires, struggles, and cultural values. We can then offer even more agency because we know them better and trust them more.

Keen observation comes from the Learning Through Observation and Pitching In (LOPI) research conducted by scholars throughout the world. This research has found that children in many Indigenous communities learn and contribute by observing and giving keen attention to what is going on around them. Visit http://learningbyobservingandpitchingin.sites.ucsc.edu to see videos of young children using their keen observation and to learn more about LOPI.

Documenting Agency

Anecdotal observations and authentic assessments are useful ways to document children's individual and communal capabilities, such as the ones described in the previous section. (See "Being a Keen Observer of Young Children" on page 27.) In addition to the formal assessments and benchmarks required by the state, Ms. Bailey included her observations about children's capabilities in the portfolios she kept for each child. She also used anecdotal notes to document academic skills, her students' interests and wonderings, and information shared by families and other caregivers pertaining to their children's interests, strengths, and developing capabilities. Observations of children's agency supplemented formal and informal assessment tools. Not only did they help Ms. Bailey authentically and strategically assess multiple skills and knowledge across disciplines, they also informed her lesson planning.

Conclusion

While agency is not a prescriptive framework, there are certain markers that are observable and can indicate the breadth and depth of the agentic experiences children are afforded in school. We have learned from partnerships with educators that when they receive support in recognizing and intentionally creating opportunities for children's agentic learning, they themselves are empowered to offer a wider variety of educational experiences that welcome children's multiple ways of learning. They become skilled in connecting curriculum to children's existing knowledge, and they prioritize the development of exploration and critical skills over teacher-centered, standardized, and narrow learning expectations.

As a field, we need to get better at observing, recognizing, and documenting children's strengths and capabilities. We also need to advocate for and create the types of agentic learning contexts that allow young children to show their full range of capabilities, interests, and knowledge. Instead of constantly trying to "fix" children—especially children of color—we must examine how disparities in systems and bias in ourselves deny young children their agency. Children cannot show and develop a range of talents and skills when they are consistently denied opportunities to move, talk, tell stories, take initiative, create projects, experiment, and work through conflicts. All children deserve to see themselves as capable learners and contributors to their communities.

Reflection Questions

1. Review "Assessing a Learning Context for Agency" on page 25. What items on this list are areas of strength already in your classroom? What would you build on and adapt in your classroom?
2. How do you see young children using their agency to learn in your classroom? What capabilities and skills do you see children demonstrate when they are using their agency?
3. What do you notice children being curious about and how do you support their curiosity? How might increasing children's agency help support curiosity and learning?
4. Provide an example of how you could create opportunities for children to have more agency in your classroom.
5. What obstacles make it difficult to support children's agency? What prevents you from supporting children's agency in your classroom in the way that you would like? What policy, program, or structural change could empower you to create and sustain an agentic learning context?

REFERENCES

Adair, J.K. 2014. "Agency and Expanding Capabilities in Early Grade Classrooms: What It Could Mean for Young Children." *Harvard Educational Review* 84 (2): 217–41.

Adair, J.K., & K.S. Colegrove. 2021. *Segregation by Experience: Agency, Racism, and Learning in the Early Grades.* Chicago: University of Chicago Press.

Adair, J.K., & S. Sachdeva. 2021. "Agency and Power in Young Children's Lives: Five Ways to Advocate for Social Justice as an Early Childhood Educator." *Young Children* 76 (2): 40–48.

Bassok, D., S. Latham, & A. Rorem. 2016. "Is Kindergarten the New First Grade?" *AERA Open* 2 (1).

Blessing, A.D. 2019. "Assessment in Kindergarten." *Young Children* 74 (3): 6–13.

Boykin, A.W., & P. Noguera. 2011. *Creating the Opportunity to Learn: Moving from Research to Practice to Close the Achievement Gap.* Alexandria, VA: ASCD.

Carr, M., & W. Lee. 2012. *Learning Stories: Constructing Learner Identities in Early Education.* London: SAGE.

Cervantes-Soon, C.G., E.D. Degollado, & I. Nuñez. 2020. "The Black and Brown Search for Agency: African American and Latinx Children's Plight to Bilingualism in a Two-Way Dual Language Program." In *Bilingualism for All? Raciolinguistic Perspectives on Dual Language Education in the United States,* eds. N. Flores, A. Tseng, & N. Subtirelu, 199–219. Bristol: Multilingual Matters.

Darling-Hammond, L., & J. Snyder. 2000. "Authentic Assessment of Teaching in Context." *Teaching and Teacher Education* 16 (5): 523–45.

Early, D.E., U.I. Iruka, S. Ritchie, O.A. Barbarin, D.M. Winn, G.M. Crawford, P.M. Frome, R.M. Clifford, M.B. Howes, D.M. Bryant, & R.C. Pianta. 2010. "How Do Pre-Kindergarteners Spend Their Time? Gender, Ethnicity, and Income as Predictors of Experiences in Pre-kindergarten Classrooms." *Early Childhood Research Quarterly* 25 (2): 177–93.

Gopnik, A. 2012. "Scientific Thinking in Young Children: Theoretical Advances, Empirical Research, and Policy Implications." *Science* 337 (6102): 1623–27.

Helm, J.H., & L. Katz. 2016. *Young Investigators: The Project Approach in the Early Years.* New York: Teachers College Press.

McManus, M.E., K. Payne, S. Lee, S. Sachdeva, A. Falkner, K. Colegrove, & J. Adair. 2019. "Expanding Video Cued Multivocal Ethnography for Activist Research in the Civic Action and Young Children Study." *Anthropology & Education Quarterly* 50 (3): 348–55.

Muller, M., E.G. Braden, S. Long, G.S. Boutte, & K. Wynter-Hoyte. 2022. "Toward Pro-Black Early Childhood Teacher Education." *Young Children* 77 (1): 44–51.

NAEYC. 2019. "Advancing Equity in Early Childhood Education." Position statement. Washington, DC: NAEYC. www.naeyc.org/resources/position-statements/equity.

NAEYC. 2020. "Developmentally Appropriate Practice." Position statement. Washington, DC: NAEYC. www.naeyc.org/resources/position-statements/dap.

Paris, D. 2012. "Culturally Sustaining Pedagogy: A Needed Change in Stance, Terminology, and Practice." *Educational Researcher* 41 (3): 93–97.

Park, S., L. Sunmin, M. Alonzo, & J.K. Adair. 2021. "Reconceptualizing Assistance for Young Children of Color with Disabilities in an Inclusion Classroom." *Topics in Early Childhood Special Education* 41 (1): 57–68.

Payne, K.A., J.K. Adair, K.S. Colegrove, S. Lee, A. Falkner, M. McManus, & S. Sachdeva. 2020. "Reconceptualizing Civic Education for Young Children: Recognizing Embodied Civic Action." *Education, Citizenship, and Social Justice* 15 (1): 35–46.

Payne, K.A., A. Falkner, & J.K. Adair. 2020. "Critical Geography in Preschool: Evidence of Early Childhood Civic Action and Ideas About Justice." *Teachers College Record* 122 (7): 1–34.

Souto-Manning, M. 2014. "Making a Stink About the 'Ideal' Classroom: Theorizing and Storying Conflict in Early Childhood Education." *Urban Education* 49 (6): 607–63.

Souto-Manning, M., B. Falk, D. López, L.B. Cruz, N. Bradt, N. Cardwell, N. McGowan, A. Perez, A. Rabadi-Raol, & E. Rollins. 2019. "A Transdisciplinary Approach to Equitable Teaching in Early Childhood Education." *Review of Research in Education* 43 (1): 249–76.

Wright, B.L. 2021. "What About the Children? Teachers Cultivating and Nurturing the Voice and Agency of Young Children." *Young Children* 76 (2): 28–32.

About the Authors

Natacha Ndabahagamye Jones is a PhD candidate in early childhood education in the Department of Curriculum and Instruction at the University of Texas at Austin. Her teaching experience as a bilingual and ESL elementary school teacher guides her research to center on the brilliance, joy, ingenuity, multiplicity, and range of capabilities young children demonstrate as they engage in knowledge-making and various other community engagements in school. She examines how systemic curricular demands intersect with early childhood educators' ability to support or disallow liberatory, agentic, and culturally sustaining educational practices, especially in communities of color that have historically been marginalized.

Amber T. Fowler, MEd, is a doctoral student in the Early Childhood Curriculum and Instruction Department at the University of Texas at Austin. Amber has taught kindergarten for six years, is studying early childhood teaching practices, and is interested in children's early childhood experiences.

Jennifer Keys Adair, PhD, is professor of early childhood education and director of the Agency and Young Children Research Collective at the University of Texas at Austin. Dr. Adair is an expert on the impact of agency and racism on young children's learning and development.

Photographs: pp. 20, 25, 26, courtesy of the authors

Strategies for Observing and Assessing

PART TWO

The next step in the assessment process is selecting the best strategy to observe and assess children (Moses 2023). In order to do this, educators must think about the audience and what story they want to tell. The data help to tell that story. For example, if administrators want to show reading progress, they may want the teacher to collect a series of observations with photos to show growth of a skill.

The six articles in this part support teachers and administrators in using various developmentally appropriate strategies to collect and evaluate data for assessment of young children.

"Authentic Assessment: A Strengths-Based Approach to Making Thinking, Learning, and Development Visible," by **Hilary Seitz,** defines authentic assessment, covers what types of artifacts and documentation can be collected as part of this process, and overviews how to share this data with others, all while using a four-step framework.

In "Anecdotal Records: Practical Strategies for Taking Meaningful Notes," **Celeste C. Bates, Stephanie M. Madison,** and **Hayley J. Hoover** take a deep dive into specific strategies and ideas to collect anecdotal records to tell the whole story of a child.

Rebecca Parlakian's article, "Bringing Observation and Documentation to Life in Infant and Toddler Settings," shares insight into how meaningful observations and data collection play an important role in the classroom and program. She offers a three-step process to analyze and act on data.

Christine M. Snyder and **Holly P. Delgado** then describe coaching strategies for teachers that are informed by and support successful assessment practices. Their article, "Unlocking the Potential of Data-Driven Coaching: Child Assessment Evidence as a Guide for Informing Instructional Practices," also provides implementation, reflection, and feedback tips.

"Effective Kindergarten Readiness Assessments: Influencing Policy, Informing Instruction, and Creating Joyful Classrooms," by **Elliot Regenstein, Maia C. Connors, Rio Romero-Jurado,** and **Joyce Weiner,** explores flexible use of mandated assessment for kindergartners. The authors discuss kindergarten readiness, when and how it is measured, and how teachers can prepare for it—all while cultivating joyful learning experiences for children.

The last article in this part is "Photographs and Learning Progressions: Supports for Intentional Assessment and Instruction in Mathematics," by **Sarah Roller Dyess, Elizabeth Petit Cunningham,** and **Katherine Ariemma Marin.** This article shares how to use photographs in the assessment cycle to document mathematical learning and show how children are progressing in their mathematical thinking and strategies.

REFERENCE

Moses, A. 2023. "Developmentally Appropriate Assessment Practices: Gathering, Understanding, and Using Information." *Young Children* 78 (1): 4–5.

Authentic Assessment

A Strengths-Based Approach to Making Thinking, Learning, and Development Visible

Hilary Seitz

Close your eyes and imagine a child walking on a playground. There are flowers in large pots in the center; around the flowerpots are gravel pathways with trees lining the edges. Beyond the trees are other children playing, talking, running, and laughing. Open your eyes and think about what you saw in your mind. Did you notice the child's facial expressions? Were they tentative about joining in with the other children, or were they excited and ready to explore on their own?

Did you notice their walking gait or other motor movements? Did you notice the different physical elements in the playground environment and how the child interacted with them? Did you notice how the child engaged with other children in their play? Did you see the outdoor environment and how it supports various areas of development and curriculum?

Learning to really see each individual child—their abilities, their strengths, and their possibilities—is an art. Documenting this and making thinking, learning, and development visible help early childhood educators understand the child better and help others value the child's capabilities. Documentation takes practice, collaboration, and support. It also takes an internal motivation to truly understand children.

In this article, I discuss how learning to use authentic assessment strategies (such as documentation of a child's skills and interests) starts with learning to see and observe children in their environments and continues with a teacher's evaluation and reflection. I also discuss the role of technology in documentation and in creating and using ePortfolios. Finally, I address how working to understand a child's community, traditions, family, and background strengthens assessment and helps to tell the child's whole story in an inclusive way.

What Is Authentic Assessment?

Authentic assessment is the process of learning about a child's capabilities, including where they are and where they are going. These capabilities include the skills, attributes, characteristics, and dispositions that help teachers understand children in their educational settings. Authentic assessment is thoughtful and intentional, requiring adequate time and resources for support. The process of authentic assessment helps to tell the "whole story" of a child, including their developmental and cultural story, their thinking story, and their group story, or how a child interacts within a group.

Authentic Assessment Strategies Are Strengths-Based

The process of authentic assessment helps to shift the concept of assessment from a narrow view of comparing children with numbers that reflect what they *do not* know to a system that demonstrates what children *do* know and can do (Escamilla 2021). One way to document visual and auditory evidence of a child's growth and learning abilities is to create a portfolio, hard copy or digital, that includes photos, transcripts, and videos (Derman-Sparks, LeeKeenan, & Nimmo 2015; Seitz 2018). To do this, teachers need an ongoing system to collect documentation (observations, photos, and work samples) on each child. For example, to document a child's ability to write, an educator can begin by collecting a writing sample with a photo of how the child holds the writing implement as well as notes about the experience. This provides assessment data for a particular date. If this process is repeated every month or two and then put together, these pieces will tell a story, and the documentation (authentic assessment) will show how the child is growing and developing.

Authentic Assessment Strategies Are Culturally Responsive

Hammond (2014) defines *culturally responsive teaching* as "an educator's ability to recognize students' cultural displays of learning and meaning making and respond positively and constructively with teaching moves that use cultural knowledge as a scaffold to connect what the student knows to new concepts and content" (15). Culturally responsive means that early educators learn about, build upon, and provide opportunities to understand children and their families. Being culturally responsive includes learning about family values and cultural traditions so that the environment is a safe and inviting place that reflects the learning community. The learning community consists of many parts that make a whole. Each group of children looks and acts differently depending on their prior knowledge and their families' experiences and expectations. When the teacher looks at these elements holistically and builds opportunities based on a group's assets, the community of learners comes together and is culturally relevant to the children and their families.

Making Learning Visible

Making learning visible involves using documentation to tell the story of the whole child and all their capabilities. The approach took root in the late 1990s and 2000s from both Harvard Graduate School of Education's initiative, Project Zero, and from John Hattie's work in New Zealand (Hattie 2009; Project Zero, Harvard Graduate School of Education, n.d.). Reggio Emilia educators also apply the model of making learning visible when using documentation and reflection to highlight learning and connections (Giudici & De Poi 2020).

Making learning visible has gained ground over the years because it is a way to deepen the understanding of children's development by using documentation as evidence. These artifacts are a form of authentic assessment and may include photographs, video clips, observation records, reflections, and work samples, all of which help to deepen the understanding of an event and to extend children's learning.

This approach helps to gather information to understand and assess individual children's learning and can also be used to reflect on group events and to tell a group's story. Group stories allow teachers to reflect on the curriculum so that they can strengthen and change learning experiences to address individual and group interests, strengths, areas of growth, and social and cultural contexts. In addition, documentation showcases everyday experiences in early childhood settings and provides meaning and value to a wide range of activities.

Authentic Assessment Strategies Promote Equity in a Digital World

Technology is all around us. We use smart phones, tablets, video games, computers, and smart speakers that talk to us. However, not all children, families, early childhood educators, and early learning programs have equitable opportunities to learn about and use technology. The issue of access became even more prominent during the COVID-19 pandemic. Some programs, educators, and families had ample technology resources to connect and engage in learning experiences, while others did not and struggled to do so, resulting in inequitable experiences and longer-term consequences (Roth 2020). Being aware of and addressing such inequities along with the purpose and intentionality of technology can help create greater equity in a digital world (Fantozzi 2022).

How can technology, such as apps, social media platforms, and websites, support authentic assessment when the digital landscape is not equitable for everyone? Teachers need to teach *how* to find, process, and use the information learned through these sources in a responsible and equitable way (Rogow 2022). Relevant and important skills for young children to learn in digitally driven learning experiences are similar to skills educators should look for in nondigital learning experiences.

These include collaboration, critical thinking, creative problem solving, and communication, which can prepare young children for current and future learning. Teachers can document this learning through multiple avenues as part of the authentic assessment process.

How Do We Make Thinking, Learning, and Development Visible?

There are four steps in the authentic assessment cycle, which are illustrated in the "Authentic Assessment Cycle" graphic on this page. The complete cycle makes learning visible in an appealing way that is culturally and linguistically appropriate and addresses how children learn in a digital world. When an educator applies these four steps, it helps various audiences in addition to the educator—including children, families, and the community—understand and value children's thinking, learning, and development.

Authentic Assessment Cycle

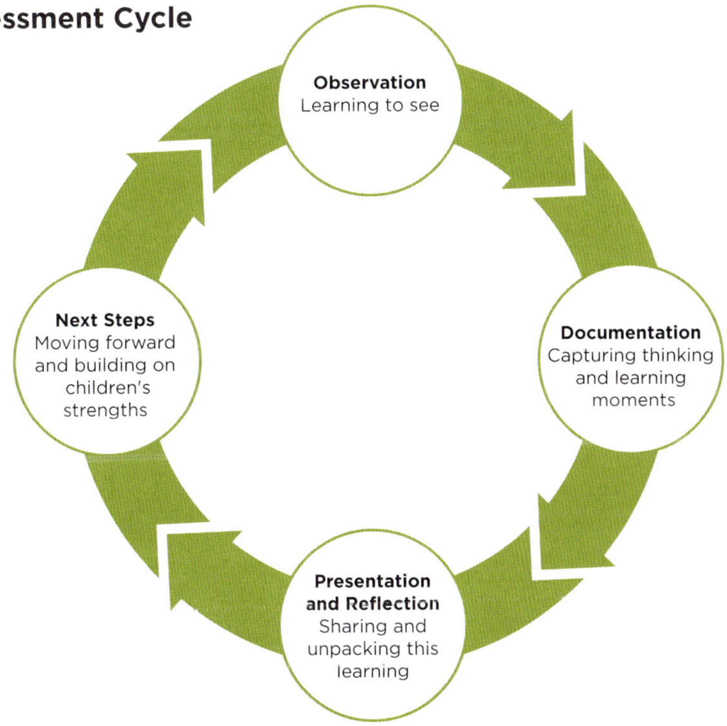

Step 1: What Can Educators Observe?

The first step in the cycle is *observation*. Observation, which serves several purposes, includes looking for thinking, learning, development, and engagement. Based on observations, teachers can plan learning experiences; respond to children's interests, strengths, and needs; decide how to guide interactions and play; and offer evidence of children's learning and development. Educators must practice watching children in and outside of educational settings. They can take photographs and videos of children engaged in activities and write down quotations of individual children, noticing and capturing small things about each child. Some of the smallest things are important, such as how often the child shares materials with a peer or where and how the child stands or sits in relation to other children or adults. It is important to note that these observations should be factual and not based on interpretations. All of us come with various preconceived ideas and different cultural lenses, so we need to observe carefully, with thoughtfulness and reflection.

Step 2: How Does Documentation Tell a Story of Learning?

After careful observation, the early childhood educator begins the second step in the cycle—*documentation*. Documentation involves looking at observational notes, records, photographs, and other collected materials. (See "What Documentation and Artifacts Should I Collect and Share?" on page 37.) Educators can put these materials together to tell the child's learning story. Documentation can take many forms, from a notebook to an ePortfolio to a website or another platform (such as a private share site accessible only to the children's families), and it can include photos, short videos, or comments about a child's learning community.

It is important to think about the audience for the documentation. If the audience is the family, teachers should provide documentation in an accessible format for the family to see their child's story. Different devices manage documentation in various ways. Administrators and community members may want to learn about different aspects of a story. For example, they may want to know how a classroom community as a whole is successful, engaged, learning, growing, and meeting developmental milestones rather than a specific child. Often, a website can make learning visible in a classroom without identifying individual children. In all cases, the educator must communicate their ideas to families beforehand and seek permission, particularly for posting photos, videos, and other personalized information.

What Documentation and Artifacts Should I Collect and Share?

Documentation and artifacts help to tell the story of a child's learning. Multiple forms of documentation and artifacts can be used to make children's thinking, learning, and development visible and to provide a fuller picture of a child's growth. In addition, they can be aligned with ongoing planning and teaching and with developmental guidelines or standards for an early learning setting.

Work Samples

Work samples are a great way to show how a child's learning and development change over time. For example, collecting writing samples at the beginning of the year and each month will show the child's progression in this area. Children's reflections on their growth through work samples can also provide a deeper understanding of their abilities. Other forms of work samples include pieces from inquiry-based projects (documentation of the process and products of the project), observational science drawings, notes from math journals, and more (Helm, Beneke, & Steinheimer 2007).

Photographs and Video Documentation

Photographs and videos can be powerful documentation tools. Children interact with materials, each other, and their teachers in ways that are sometimes hard to write about or to record on a checklist or rating sheet. Many children are familiar with being photographed and recorded, and families like these tools too. Building on technologies already familiar to children and families and sharing these forms of documentation are easy ways to make learning visible (Seitz 2018; Seitz & Bartholomew 2008).

Seeing interactions of children engaged in their learning through short video clips and photographs—like a clip of a child building a block tower or a photograph of a child holding a pencil and a second photo showing the writing sample—helps to tell a more comprehensive story. In addition, when educators add information about why the events in video clips and photographs are important, the evidence can be compelling to share through an ePortfolio.

Observational Records

An *observational record* is an authentic notation about an occurrence in an early childhood setting. Observational records can capture moments like a child learning to write their name or learning how to balance on one foot. Teachers can write observations on sticky notes, in a handy notebook, or on a more formalized sheet. More recently, some teachers and programs have started to use an app to record observational notes. Written and typed notes can be uploaded to an ePortfolio collection.

Resources

Resources can be added to portfolios to make them a richer, more supportive experience. Embedded resources, like state standards, school district guidelines, and program guidelines, may be hyperlinked to support documentation throughout the portfolio. Resources may also entail enhancements or extension ideas for families connected to projects or learning experiences, like book suggestions for related children's books and ideas for family adventures such as taking a walk down a neighborhood street to find five different color houses or buildings.

A final section in the portfolio may include local community resources and events. This is an easy way to help families connect to the services and supports such as local recreation and cultural centers, physical and mental health agencies, nutrition services or programs, and more.

Step 3: How Can Educators Showcase the Value of Learning Experiences with Families and Communities?

The third step in the cycle is *presentation and reflection*. This is important for educators, children, families, and the community because sharing and unpacking the documentation of learning help to underscore the value and purpose of the learning experiences. Presentation and reflection can be done in several formats; each has value in a different way. A presentation may be as simple as welcoming a family into the classroom at the end of the day and inviting the child to share a sample from their ePortfolio or a piece of their work displayed on a bulletin board. Having a child become the center of the experience tells them that their work, abilities, and ideas are important and special.

Teachers may facilitate a more formal gathering or family celebration to share documentation of a group's collective work. Formal sharing can be done in the evening, during class lunch, or even during the weekend, depending on a family or community member's access and schedules. The actual event can be presented by educators and children through a video or a series of documentation panels. A documentation panel showcases photographs, written transcripts, and work samples as a story on a bulletin board or on smaller poster panels.

These sharings celebrate the children's strengths, imaginations, and abilities. Formal presentation gatherings are also outlets for families to build a sense of community based on their children's learning and cultural connections. After the presentation, it is important to reflect on the experience. This leads to the last step of the process.

Step 4: How Does Authentic Assessment Inform Future Learning?

The *next steps* portion, the fourth and final step in the authentic assessment cycle, helps educators determine where a child is developmentally and emotionally and consider what to do next. For example, do some children need more time with building blocks? Are others ready to take the next step toward writing sight words? Teachers and families can answer these questions together as they look at children's authentic assessments and build a curriculum in response. In this way, the curriculum will be more meaningful and more connected to children and their families, their communities, and cultural values.

Reflection Questions

1. What are some ways that you make children's learning visible in your classroom?
2. If your early learning program uses a digital assessment system, how do you share it with families? If you don't use a digital system, what types of technology would help you to make learning visible?
3. What types of artifacts and other documentation do you collect in your classroom? How do you or could you share these so the whole learning community can see the children's learning and growth?
4. How do you tell the "whole story" of a child to share all of their strengths alongside of their needs?

Conclusion

The authentic assessment process is a valuable tool in today's diverse early childhood classroom. Learning to observe, document, and present and reflect guides teachers to the final progression, next steps, which is needed to help children grow and thrive. Authentic assessment helps build community in the classroom and is a way to really know and understand each child's cultural and learning story.

REFERENCES

Derman-Sparks, L., D. LeeKeenan, & J. Nimmo. 2015. *Leading Anti-Bias Early Childhood Programs: A Guide for Change*. New York: Teachers College Press; Washington, DC: NAEYC.

Escamilla, I.M. 2021. "Learning Stories: Observation, Reflection, and Narrative in Early Childhood Education." In *Advancing Equity and Embracing Diversity in Early Childhood Education: Elevating Voices and Actions,* eds. I. Alanís & I.U. Iruka, with S. Friedman, 94–97. Washington, DC: NAEYC.

Fantozzi, V.B. 2022. *Digital Tools for Learning, Creating, and Thinking: Developmentally Appropriate Strategies for Early Childhood Educators*. Washington, DC: NAEYC.

Giudici, C., & S. De Poi. 2020. "Making Learning Visible." Webinar from Reggio Children, November & December. www.reggiochildren.it/en/e-learning/webinars-and-web-conferences/making-learning-visible.

Hammond, Z. 2014. *Culturally Responsive Teaching and the Brain: Promoting Authentic Engagement and Rigor Among Culturally and Linguistically Diverse Students*. Thousand Oaks, CA: Corwin Press.

Hattie, J. 2009. *Visible Learning: A Synthesis of Over 800 Meta-Analyses Relating to Achievement*. London, UK: Routledge.

Helm, J.H., S. Beneke, & K. Steinheimer. 2007. *Windows on Learning: Documenting Young Children's Work*. 2nd ed. New York: Teachers College Press.

Project Zero, Harvard Graduate School of Education. n.d. "Making Learning Visible." Accessed November 29, 2022. https://pz.harvard.edu/projects/making-learning-visible.

Rogow, F. 2022. *Media Literacy for Young Children: Teaching Beyond the Screen Time Debates*. Washington, DC: NAEYC.

Roth, K. 2020. "Technology in Education: The Ongoing Debate of Access, Adequacy and Equity." Master's diss, Bank Street College of Education. https://educate.bankstreet.edu/independent-studies/248.

Seitz, H. 2018. "The Power of Documentation in the Early Childhood Classroom." In *Spotlight on Young Children: Observation and Assessment,* eds. H. Bohart & R. Procopio, 50–57. Washington, DC: NAEYC.

Seitz, H., & C. Bartholomew. 2008. "Powerful Portfolios for Young Children." *Early Childhood Education Journal* 36 (1): 63–68.

About the Author

Hilary Seitz, PhD, is director for educator and leadership programs in the California State University system. She advocates and supports statewide efforts to support early childhood education and the new California PK–Early Childhood Education Specialist Instruction Credential. Dr. Seitz is professor emerita in early childhood education at the University of Alaska Anchorage. Her research areas have been in early literacy development, collaborative practices between families and schools including culturally responsive pedagogies, emergent curriculum development, documentation, authentic assessment, and social constructivist learning theories inspired by Reggio Emilia practices.

This article is partially adapted from H. Seitz, "Making Thinking, Learning, and Development Visible and Inclusive Through Authentic Assessment," in *Advancing Equity and Embracing Diversity in Early Childhood Education: Elevating Voices and Actions*, eds. I. Alanís & I.U. Iruka, with S. Friedman (Washington, DC: NAEYC, 2021), 90–93.

Anecdotal Records

Practical Strategies for Taking Meaningful Notes

Celeste C. Bates, Stephanie M. Madison, and Hayley J. Hoover

For many teachers, the word *assessment* conjures up negative feelings. High-stakes, *summative assessments* are used to gauge student learning against a standard or a benchmark (Afflerbach 2016; Ferguson 2017) and are sometimes used to make significant educational decisions about children. Largely because of this pressure, school districts across the country now require benchmark assessments two or more times during the school year to track students' progress. With so many mandated assessments, teachers often feel they have no time to teach.

Although these fall and winter benchmark tests are intended to be *formative assessments* that help guide instruction, many teachers don't find them to be very helpful. For example, in a recent conversation, a first-grade teacher lamented that six weeks into the school year she had yet to begin working with small groups in her classroom. While she recognized that some of the delay related to getting classroom routines and procedures under way, she also clearly stated, "All I ever seem to do is assess my children, and the information doesn't even help me plan instruction." Though this may seem a little extreme, her feelings are shared by teachers nationwide (Saeki et al. 2018).

Benchmark assessments often have a narrow focus and rigid procedures and, as a result, do not capture children's true knowledge and skills. In contrast, formative assessments monitor children's learning and provide ongoing checks of student progress that allow teachers to "plan and adapt curriculum to meet each child's developmental and learning needs" (Copple & Bredekamp 2009, 321).

Formative assessment is theoretically intended to bring together three fundamental processes: (1) determining where children are in their learning; (2) understanding the developmental continuum and educational expectations; and (3) charting a course to support children's progress (Black & Wiliam 2009; Hattie & Timperley 2007). Formative assessments are often embedded in the daily activities "undertaken by teachers and/or by their students, which provide information to be used as feedback to modify the teaching and learning activities in which they are engaged" (Black & Wiliam 1998, 7).

For teachers, the most useful formative assessments tend to be authentic in nature and look at children's performances on specific, real-life tasks (Wiggins 1990). The information gleaned from this type of assessment supports teachers in planning responsive and intentional instruction. For example, a teacher may review a child's journal entry as a form of authentic assessment to determine the child's current knowledge of capitalization and punctuation. The assessment could be used in formative (instructional planning) or summative (outcome-focused) ways, but teachers usually tend to emphasize the formative uses since their goals are to create lessons and activities that meet children's needs. In addition to examining children's journals and other products, another type of authentic assessment that is often used for formative purposes is teachers' anecdotal notes recorded during close observations of children.

Many teachers see the value of detailed anecdotal notes but have a hard time simultaneously being the teacher and the note taker. This article provides practical strategies for the use of anecdotal notes as one type of authentic assessment. The article discusses what constitutes anecdotal records and offers suggestions for taking notes efficiently; defines the notion of close observation; and examines the use of notes as part of reflective practice. Ideas for implementing and managing an anecdotal record-keeping system are also provided.

Anecdotal Records

Anecdotal records are brief notes grounded in the close observations of children (Clay 2001). The notes record a range of student behaviors in areas such as literacy, mathematics, social studies, science, the arts, social and emotional development, and physical development. When recording observations, it is important to document a behavior in terms that provide a concrete description and enough details to inform future instruction. Statements such as "the student was on task" provide no information about the task or the behavior.

To avoid vague notes, list the associated learning center or subject area, and include specific information describing what the child is doing. For example, "Landon—Reading Center—selected two books from his personal book basket. Matched one-to-one, voice to print on two lines of text." The details in this note provide information about the child's independent behavior in the reading center. By stating that Landon controlled voice-to-print match, it shows that he also controls left-to-right directional movement across a line of text. Additionally, by recording that there were two lines of print, the note also indicates that Landon understands the concept of return sweep and the top-to-bottom progression of text.

To make note taking more efficient, consider using abbreviated language. Without developing a lot of complicated shorthand, the teacher could write the note above as "Landon—RC—selected 2 books from his personal book basket. Matched 1-1/V to P on 2 lines of text." Time is always a concern, and children move quickly from one task to the next. Abbreviations assist in capturing detailed observations in an efficient manner and in keeping up with the children.

In addition to using abbreviations, it is powerful to ground an observation in evidence. Instead of stating "Leah uses inventive spelling," the anecdotal note should include evidence of her inventive spelling: "Leah—DP [Dramatic Play]—Wrote grocery list: BACN, aGS, sreL." The evidence provides insight into the consonants and vowels Leah is learning and the letter forms she can produce. Additionally, the evidence aids the teacher in better understanding Leah's progress on the learning trajectory toward standard spelling and the teacher is more informed about how to support her instructionally.

Capturing evidence in the form of an anecdotal note can sometimes be difficult. It may be easier to collect and copy a child's artifact or work sample and save it alongside the anecdotal record. Another option is to take a photograph of the artifact and embed it and the accompanying anecdotal record in the child's portfolio (Bates 2014).

Finally, when taking anecdotal records, it is important for teachers to consider their word choices and the ways in which the use of certain language may inadvertently position students in teachers' minds. Statements that begin with words like *can't* or *doesn't* promote a deficit view and do not assist with future instructional planning. For example, making the statement "Logan doesn't identify all his letters" is very different from saying "Logan identifies the letters A, B, G, N, L, T, Z." Writing what children *can* do ensures the teacher's instructional decisions are grounded in students' strengths.

Close Observation

To take meaningful and useful anecdotal notes, teachers must first adopt the role of observer. Teachers are in a unique position to closely observe children's behaviors and conversations and to capture these observations in writing (Boyd-Batstone 2004). The quality of anecdotal notes depends on a teacher's ability to be a neutral observer in order to record behaviors that "inform a teacher's . . . understanding of cognitive processes" (232). Subconscious assumptions and biases must be checked at the door.

It is easy to draw conclusions about a child, especially when a teacher has a history with the family, such as previously teaching a sibling. No two children are exactly alike, even if they share the same family, community, and/or culture. Familiarity with children and families may assist in developing the home-school connection, but it should not predetermine the way a child is viewed. Similarly, familiarity with a child's community or culture may provide informative context, but it should not lead to making assumptions—positive or negative.

Anecdotal records are intended to be neutral observations of a child's behaviors and interactions. The observations may be simple, such as the way the child handles a book, distinguishing the front from the back, or complex, such as the way a child works through a disagreement with a peer on the playground. Regardless, it is imperative to remain impartial when describing and recording what is observed. While this may seem obvious, it is important to guard against assumptions and biases that can creep into written observations.

Periodically, teachers should review their notes to look for examples of bias. They may reflect on ways the notes have been written to see if they are objective and provide details about the child's actions and demonstrated behaviors. Teachers may also look for patterns in their notes to see if subjective comments are linked to any one child or to a group of children. Identifying these patterns can help reveal unconscious assumptions and support teachers' objectivity in future observations. Finally, teachers may also ask a trusted colleague to review their notes for the same purposes.

Organizing and Managing Anecdotal Records

One of the biggest challenges for educators is managing the many demands on their time (Sparapani & Perez 2015). Therefore, it is incredibly important to establish a system for taking and using anecdotal records that is easy to implement and stick to. For the system to become a seamlessly integrated part of the day, organization is key. With a clear approach, teachers can take and use daily anecdotal notes as a means of formative assessment to guide instruction. The thought of doing one more thing might seem overwhelming to some teachers, but it does not have to be.

Daily anecdotal notes can be quick to write and easy to file and organize and should serve as the basis for reflective practice. By monitoring each child's development with daily anecdotal notes and adjusting instructional support accordingly, teachers' perceptions of assessment often shift from assessment for assessment's sake to assessment for the sake of children's learning and growth.

When taking anecdotal records, it is important to be selective about the behaviors being observed. Depending on the needs of a particular class, a teacher may choose to focus only on reading and writing behaviors (instead of on an array of behaviors). Having a specific focus helps teachers attend to the most important details during observations, making anecdotal records more meaningful and actionable for planning or individualizing future instruction. In addition, it removes the unreasonable expectation of documenting everything for every student, every day.

One suggestion for getting started is to divide the class into small groups of approximately five students. Once the groups are established, assign each group a day of the week, and then concentrate on observing just those five students on their day. These *daily focus groups* are a good way to organize and manage record keeping—and they prevent children from slipping through the cracks. The following are three examples of anecdotal record-keeping systems that use daily focus groups.

Post-It Notebook

A Post-it notebook uses a form for each student that has six boxes. Teachers often choose to label the boxes *Reading, Writing, Math, Science/Social Studies, Social/Emotional,* and *Other,* but the form can be tailored to highlight any content areas or learning domains that a teacher chooses. As observations are made, they are recorded on a Post-it Note, or sticky note, and placed on a clipboard. At the end of the day, the notes are transferred to the child's form and are placed in the appropriate category. The forms are kept in a three-ring binder with dividers separating each daily focus group.

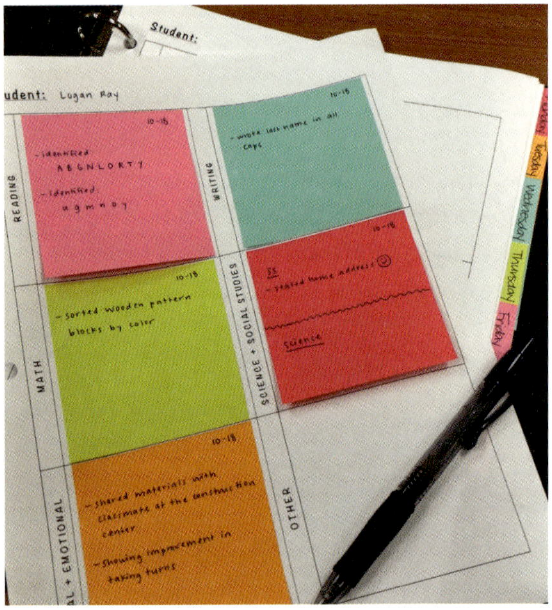

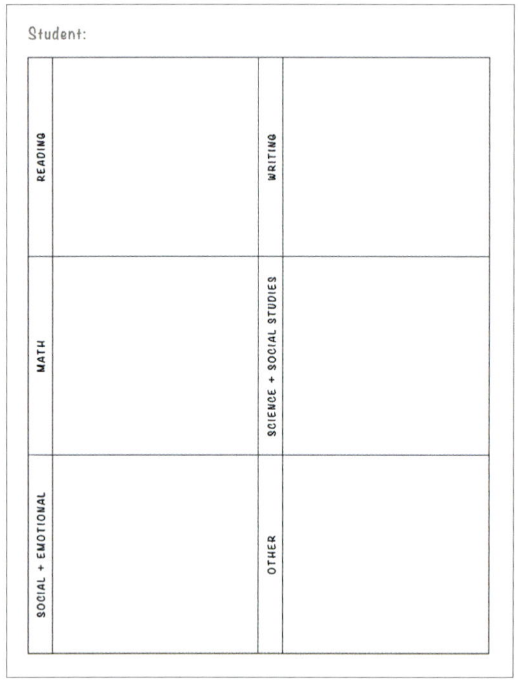

Index Cards

The index card system uses individual index cards, color coded by daily focus group (Monday's group is assigned green index cards, and Tuesday's group is yellow). A binder clip is used to keep each group's index cards together. The cards are used throughout the day as the teacher captures and records observations on the group members' individual cards. At the end of the day, the cards are filed in a box, and then the cards for the next day are pulled.

Teachers may choose to record literacy behaviors (or any other content area they are emphasizing) on one side of the card and math behaviors (or another content area) on the other side. Additional cards can be used to capture behaviors in other areas, or the card can be subdivided. Once a child's card is completely full of anecdotal observations, a new card is issued. In addition to using the cards in the classroom, teachers can easily take them outdoors when observing and recording students' social interactions on the playground.

Bookmarks

Bookmarks are a variation of anecdotal notes used specifically when conferencing with children about literacy. Anecdotal observations made by the teacher are integrated into the conference in the form of goals for a student's reading, and student and teacher together then discuss strategies for achieving those goals. For example, the anecdotal observation on the teacher's part may be "Sophia—reads one word at a time while pointing to each word." As a result of this observation, the goal for Sophia would be fluent reading with appropriate pauses, and the strategy would be to have her practice reading without pointing to the words.

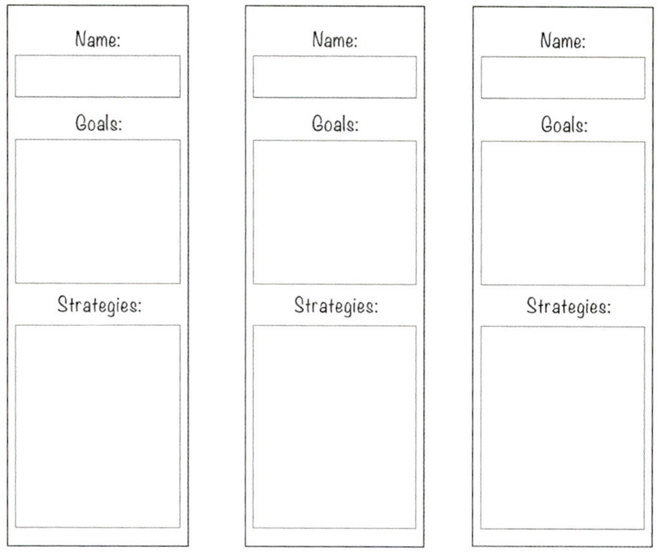

The bookmark displays actionable items discussed with the child that result from the teacher's close observation. For convenience, the back of the bookmark can be used to house the anecdotal records that are linked to the student's goals and the suggested strategies. Each time the teacher and child have a conference, the bookmark is used to check on the child's progress, to record additional observations, and to modify and adjust the child's goals and strategies, as needed.

Reflecting and Using Anecdotal Notes

Once a manageable system is in place, teachers have the information they need to reflect about what the children are learning. Reflection and anecdotal notes should be inextricably linked and serve as the foundation for instructional planning, helping teachers think more deeply about their students' growth and learning. Furthermore, reflecting on these records allows teachers to generate questions and hypotheses that fuel additional observations and anecdotal records, making this type of formative assessment "ongoing, strategic, and purposeful" (Copple & Bredekamp 2009, 22).

Reflection on formative assessments allows teachers to ensure that important, in-the-moment observations not only get recorded but are used to understand children's individual accomplishments (Afflerbach 2016). Adopting a child-centered approach to assessment ensures students are viewed from a strengths-based perspective and teaching is matched to individuals' needs. As a result, children receive more tailored instruction as teachers are better informed about each child's progress. Reflecting on anecdotal notes can also assist with grouping decisions. Small groups within the classroom should be flexible; using observational data assists teachers in re-forming groups to mirror children's changing needs.

A daily habit of reflection can be hard to develop, but as teachers organize and manage the notes they take during the day, they can review them and draw conclusions that support instructional decisions. If finding time daily is difficult, setting aside a portion of a planning period at the end of the week is another way to intentionally reflect on children's progress.

Many teachers find it useful to write out their reflections and add them to the collection of anecdotal records on a child; as months go by, being able to review both anecdotal notes and timely reflections can be very informative. Additionally, the information gleaned from the anecdotal records can be transferred to more formal assessments, like developmental checklists. When a challenging situation arises, such as a child not making progress as expected, it may be helpful for the teacher to share notes and reflections with colleagues to generate new ideas about lessons and activities to try. And if a comprehensive or diagnostic assessment seems called for, the teacher has a rich set of records to share with families and specialists.

Communication about a child's progress is important, and anecdotal notes are a rich source of information when meeting with a family. During a parent conference, anecdotal notes can be used to provide the family with concrete examples of their child's learning and development and give them insight into the child's school day. The information can also help the teacher relay to the parents ways to support the child at home. Instead of using a broad, sweeping statement to describe a child, sharing anecdotal notes during a conference and in other communications can provide a detailed description of the child's cognitive and social behaviors. These detailed descriptions, in turn, help the parents better understand their child's learning trajectory.

Conclusion

Early childhood classrooms are busy places. Capturing and deriving meaning from the behaviors of more than a handful of children can be tricky. If observations are not recorded in the moment, important details may be forgotten by the end of the day.

Developing a manageable system for taking and using anecdotal notes in the early childhood classroom is key for intentional instruction. A well-organized system frees the teacher to focus attention on the children instead of thinking about the "how to" aspects of record keeping. Notes with clear language, abbreviations, and evidence provide concrete documentation of children's emerging behaviors, knowledge, and skills, and they also ground teachers' reflective practices. It is this type of assessment, both intentional and supportive, that contributes to children's learning and development.

Reflection Questions

1. What types of formative assessments do you use to determine where children are in their learning and development? How do these formative assessments inform your planning and instruction?
2. Think about the data you collect in your classroom. Do you collect anecdotal records in addition to children's artifacts and work samples? If not, how could you integrate the process of recording anecdotal notes?
3. This article discusses several ideas for recording useful anecdotal notes, including using abbreviations and focusing on specific tasks that children perform. With a colleague or partner, brainstorm other strategies that could help you take quick but informative notes.
4. What type of organizational system do you use for compiling your notes? Are there any strategies discussed in this article that could make your system more efficient?

REFERENCES

Afflerbach, P. 2016. "Reading Assessment: Looking Ahead." *The Reading Teacher* 69 (4): 413–19.

Bates, C.C. 2014. "Digital Portfolios: Using Technology to Involve Families." *Young Children* 69 (4): 56–57.

Black, P., & D. Wiliam. 1998. "Assessment and Classroom Learning." *Assessment in Education: Principles, Policy & Practice* 5 (1): 7–74.

Black, P., & D. Wiliam. 2009. "Developing the Theory of Formative Assessment." *Educational Assessment, Evaluation and Accountability* 21 (1): 5–31.

Boyd-Batstone, P. 2004. "Focused Anecdotal Records Assessment: A Tool for Standards-Based, Authentic Assessment." *The Reading Teacher* 58 (3): 230–39.

Clay, M.M. 2001. *Change Over Time in Children's Literacy Development*. Portsmouth, NH: Heinemann.

Copple, C., & S. Bredekamp, eds. 2009. *Developmentally Appropriate Practice in Early Childhood Programs Serving Children from Birth through Age 8*. 3rd ed. Washington, DC: NAEYC.

Ferguson, K. 2017. "Using a Simulation to Teach Reading Assessment to Preservice Teachers." *The Reading Teacher* 70 (5): 561–69.

Hattie, J., & H. Timperley. 2007. "The Power of Feedback." *Review of Educational Research* 77 (1): 81–112.

Saeki, E., N. Segool, L. Pendergast, & N. von der Embse. 2018. "The Influence of Test-Based Accountability Policies on Early Elementary Teachers: School Climate, Environmental Stress, and Teacher Stress." *Psychology in the Schools* 55 (4): 391–403.

Sparapani, E.F., & D.M.C. Perez. 2015. "A Perspective on the Standardized Curriculum and Its Effect on Teaching and Learning." *Journal of Education & Social Policy* 2 (5): 78–87.

Wiggins, G. 1990. "The Case for Authentic Assessment." *Practical Assessment, Research & Evaluation* 2 (2). https://scholarworks.umass.edu/pare/vol2/iss1/2.

About the Authors

Celeste C. Bates, PhD, is professor of literacy education and the director of the Clemson University Reading Recovery and Early Literacy Center in Clemson, South Carolina.

Stephanie M. Madison, PhD, is project manager for Clemson University's Teacher Learning Progression grant, which is funded by the US Department of Education's Supporting Effective Educator Development Program. A former Spanish teacher, Stephanie studies issues of cultural and linguistic diversity.

Hayley J. Hoover, PhD, is a classroom teacher in the School District of Pickens County. Hayley has taught in special education and general education settings.

Bringing Observation and Documentation to Life in Infant and Toddler Settings

Rebecca Parlakian

Gabriella, a teacher of 2- and 3-year-olds, looks over her class list. One of her children, Harrison, is absent again today. "Hmmm," she thinks. "Nine absences this month. I hope everything's all right." She makes a note to share the attendance information with her program's family support specialist; perhaps there's a way to support Harrison's family in their efforts to get him to school.

Next, Gabriella reaches into her pocket and pulls out several sticky notes. One says "Camila, cows, vocab." She remembers how earlier in the day, Camila had pulled the cow puppet onto her hand and told a story about the cow taking a bath. "Camila's vocabulary is really taking off," Gabriella thinks. "Maybe we should read some stories about farm animals if she's interested in cows."

A quick look at the calendar reminds Gabriella that at their next meeting, staff will hear about the results from a recent program-wide observation of teacher-child interactions and classroom climate. "I wonder what that will mean for our classroom," she thinks.

Research shows that the experiences children have in early childhood influence their development and later school success. Specifically, children who experience higher quality care in early childhood are more likely to have better educational and social outcomes than children in lower quality settings. These associations persist through adolescence, shining a spotlight on the central role that early learning experiences play in children's development (La Paro, Williamson, & Hatfield 2014).

Meaningful assessment practices can help guide the selection of curriculum and instructional approaches used with very young children. These practices can also help us in our own professional journeys, providing insight into our practices, strengths, and needs. At the classroom or program level, aggregate (or combined) data can show progress toward program outcomes for children and can help staff identify professional development goals.

While early childhood educators have a wealth of choices when it comes to collecting assessment information (see "Screenings and Other Formal Assessment Tools" on this page), they most often rely on conducting and recording observations with infants and toddlers. These observations can happen quite naturally across the day—during everyday routines (drop-off, mealtimes, and naptimes) and during play. This article focuses on the steps educators can take to understand and use the information they gather.

Screenings and Other Formal Assessment Tools

Teacher observations and documentation are usually informal ways of assessing the infant and toddler environment. If concerns about a child's development arise—either from educators or the family—then a developmental screening may be in order. For example, if a toddler is consistently demonstrating repetitive behaviors, such as spinning or hand-flapping, further evaluation may be warranted.

Developmental screenings allow teachers and other professionals to formally compare a child's current skills and behaviors to a set of established norms. They include the Ages & Stages Questionnaires, BRIGANCE, and DENVER II, among others (Macy & Bagnato 2022). These screenings, typically administered by professionals outside the program, may indicate the need for a more comprehensive evaluation.

Screenings are designed to provide detailed information about a child's abilities and needs in a particular domain of development. Certain formal assessments can also be used for diagnostic purposes. Because consistent and accurate information is integral to early intervention/early special education efforts, early childhood educators can offer critical insights and details during the evaluation process. To learn more, see "Authentic and Meaningful Developmental Screening in Early Childhood," by Marisa Macy and Stefano J. Bagnato (pages 110–115 of this volume).

Bringing Information to Life in Our Work

As Patricia McDonald (2018) writes, "teachers are researchers, observing children to decide how to extend their learning both in the moment and by planning new play environments" (32). The observations infant and toddler teachers make can provide rich insights into the very young child's experiences, including

- Their interests. Where do their passions lie? (Dinosaurs? Dancing and singing? Garbage trucks?)
- Their development. Are they showing early milestones toward walking (pulling up, creeping along furniture) or toileting (signaling when they are going to have a bowel movement)?
- Their needs. Perhaps a 6-month-old cannot hold their bottle independently but can do so with support.
- Their temperament, likes, and dislikes. For example, some children may tolerate a block tower falling over and over again while others may be distressed the first time the blocks collapse.

Teachers can collect and record these observations in several ways. They may make a quick note on a sticky pad; take a video or photo; make a note in the child's chart or daily record; and/or record "frequency counts" of how often a specific behavior (like biting) is observed. Whatever system a teacher uses, it is important to partner with other staff in their setting so that everyone uses a similar approach.

Regardless of how it is gathered, assessment information—including informal observation and other, more formal practices—is meaningful only when it is understood and brought to life in the early learning program. Educators can follow a three-step process to guide how they interpret and act on the information they collect.

1. Reflection: What Does It Mean?

Early childhood educators gather information about children for a variety of reasons. They may want to track a child's development, needs, and strengths; assess a program's compliance activities; or examine their own teaching practices and classroom climate. They can observe individual children or an entire class (which is particularly helpful when tracking progress toward a specific learning objective, such as rhyming, counting, or engaging in different types of play). Once they have gathered the information, they can connect with a supervisor or other staff member, family members, or even the children who participated in the observation to identify themes and insights and to reflect on what the information means (Scott-Little with Reschke 2022). Reflection questions could include

- What does this assessment information tell me about children's learning and development?
- What does it tell me about my teaching practices?
- What can I learn about the classroom climate, including how I interact with children and how they interact with each other?
- Does this information capture how children are accessing, mastering, and applying new knowledge and skills?

2. Feedback: What Is the Context?

There is a lot going on in an early learning program at any point in time, and that context may contribute to the "story" that observation and documentation tells. For example, perhaps an observation took place after a lockdown or fire drill, so children were more distressed and unsettled than usual. Or perhaps it occurred after a new staff member joined the classroom. When analyzing observations, it is important to consider these contexts and the ways they influence what we observe. This could prompt teachers to plan for additional observation.

Knowledge of the children (and families) in our settings is another important source of feedback. Teachers should consider how culture, language, background knowledge, immigration experiences, family strengths, and more influence children's learning. This intentional awareness of each child's unique context, strengths, and needs is aligned

Sharing Assessment Information with Families

Observations are rich "moments in time" and can offer families a deeper understanding of what their children do and discover during the day. By sharing these observations during pickup time, in classroom newsletters, or during educator-family conferences, teachers can build trust and connections with the families in their settings.

Families have a right to understand what is being collected about their children, how the information is being used, and in what ways it is being shared with other staff and agencies. Because assessment can be formal or informal, specific to one child or program-wide, educators may struggle with how to meaningfully share the information they gather. Here are some guidelines for discussing data collection (Lin et al. 2016):

- Inform families about the program's assessment practices at enrollment. Explain what information the program collects, why they collect it, and how it may be used.
- Allow families to choose if they want to share personal information. This helps build trust. Programs should also outline the ways they ensure families' privacy and the data protections they have in place (such as confidentiality agreements, data sharing agreements, and secure data storage).
- Highlight the benefits of collecting assessment information. These include determining a child's eligibility for community services; documenting that children are receiving necessary services; illustrating a child's progress and learning across the curriculum; ensuring compliance with funding agencies; and guiding improvements to the program.

to developmentally appropriate practice: "The methods of assessment are responsive to the current developmental accomplishments, language(s), and experiences of young children. They recognize individual variation in learners and allow children to demonstrate their competencies in different ways" (NAEYC 2020, 20).

3. Action Planning: What Comes Next?

Once teachers collect information, they can review it regularly to identify areas of growth and areas for attention or changes they may want to make. Based on their observations, teachers can design playful learning activities that are intentional and responsive to children's interests and abilities (Head Start 2022). When planning these activities, teachers might ask themselves the following questions (Peterson & Elam 2020):

- How can I set up the environment to better meet children's needs? Do I need to change routines, materials, or schedules?
- What milestones or learning objectives can I support through planned experiences?
- What resources or materials do I need to meet these objectives?
- Do I need to consider modifications, adaptations, or other adjustments to support each and every child's meaningful participation in learning experiences?

For example, imagine that observations over time showed that teachers were engaging in fewer conversations with emergent multilingual learners compared with monolingual children (Hannon 2019). Seeing these data, teachers might assign a group of children to each staff member in the room, with the goal that adults engage each of "their" children in multiple conversations a day. At the program level, directors might decide to invest in professional development designed to enrich the language environment.

Theory and Practice

Think About It

- Consider when you've used assessment information to make a decision; for example, selecting a route for a road trip based on estimated drive times or keeping track of a child's fever to decide when to give medication.
- Most educators regularly make informal observations of the children in their setting. Think about a time you've used observations to adjust your planning or teaching.
- Reflect on your own teaching practice. Where would you like support in incorporating observational data or assessment results into your practice? What information would provide ongoing insights into your skills and progress toward your goals?

Try It

- As you review assessment information for your setting or practice, take a moment to check in with yourself. Do you have any immediate reactions (pride, satisfaction, insecurity, frustration)? It is normal to have strong feelings about assessment data. Acknowledging our feelings helps us manage them so these reactions don't get in the way of our ability to use and learn from the information.
- Look at data as a snapshot in time and one piece of a larger picture. Consider what other sources of information you may have that can add to this picture. Informal observations, children's work samples, videos, and feedback from families are all examples of other important data sources.
- Use assessment information as a jumping off point for curriculum planning. Experiment with new approaches, activities, or ways of being with children. Invite a colleague to observe you implementing these changes and to offer thoughts on how they're working.
- Share assessment information with families to help them understand planned changes to the environment or your teaching. For example, you might use a weekly newsletter to explain that you've been observing young toddlers stacking objects and knocking them down. Let families know that in the coming weeks, you will introduce different types of blocks and boxes to give children an opportunity to explore this cause-and-effect relationship with a range of materials. Ask them if they've noticed their child engaging in similar cause-and-effect behaviors.

Informal observations can also guide adult learning by providing an opportunity for teachers to reflect and consider their own professional strengths and needs. After implementing any changes, educators can plan to collect follow-up data: Did the adjustments lead to anticipated outcomes? If not, why? Is more time needed to implement the changes, or should teachers try other approaches instead?

Observation and Documentation in Action

The following vignette shows how Gabriella used the three step process in her infant and toddler classroom.

> Gabriella's class struggles with transitions, particularly when toddlers in her room prepare to go outside. She asks her colleague, Isis, to come in and observe during this time of day. Isis sees that some children are zipped up and standing by the door while other children are

Reflection Questions

1. Think about the types of screening tools you use with infants and toddlers. What type of information are you collecting? What do you learn from it? Do you collaborate with other professionals or children's families in gathering and interpreting this data? What supports do you have in place to reflect on this data and better support children in your setting?
2. How do you consider issues of culture, home language(s), and other important contexts as you reflect on observations of children in your care?
3. Think of a specific child you teach, including their interests, abilities, strengths, and needs. Create an action plan to support that child's growth and development.
4. When have you used the three-step process of reflection, feedback, and action planning? What were the results of this process?

waiting to be helped into their jackets. By the time children get outside, some are crying, others have unzipped their jackets, and one pushes a peer to get out the door.

At a follow-up meeting with Isis, Gabriella uses the three-step approach of reflection, feedback, and action planning. She **reflects** on her frustration that a seemingly "simple" transition poses such a challenge, then considers the observational data that some children are waiting up to four to five minutes in their jackets and boots by the door. Gabriella shares her goal for making the transition to the playground smoother for everyone. With Isis' help, Gabriella offers important **feedback** about the children she works with—young toddlers have difficulty waiting, yet they need adult assistance with dressing. Gabriella then focuses on **action planning**: What can be done to ease this transition?

Gabriella and her two coteachers decide to put children's coats on the backs of their chairs during snack time and to line up boots by the playground door. As the first children finish their snack, Gabriella will help them get dressed, and her two coteachers will take them to the playground. One coteacher will stay to supervise outdoor play while the other heads back to the classroom. Gabriella will remain in the room, helping each child put on jacket and boots, while her coteacher leads children to the playground individually or in small groups as they're ready. This approach cuts down children's waiting time, allows for more one-on-one attention, creates opportunities for children to practice early dressing skills, and ultimately meets Gabriella's goal of providing a calmer transition to outdoor play.

Conclusion

While most often informal, teacher and staff observations are an important contribution to effective teaching. Taking the time to understand and apply these findings creates an environment of ongoing reflection and learning—for teachers and children.

REFERENCES

Hannon, S.M. 2019. "It's Time to Shine a Light on Language Isolation in Infant and Toddler Classrooms." *Lena: Building Brains Through Early Talk,* January 15. www.lena.org/classroom-language-isolation.

Head Start Early Childhood Learning and Knowledge Center. 2022. "Child Observation: The Heart of Individualizing Responsive Care for Infants and Toddlers." Last modified June 13. https://eclkc.ohs.acf.hhs.gov/child-screening-assessment/child-observation-heart-individualizing-responsive-care-infants-toddlers/child-observation-heart-individualizing.

La Paro, K.M., A.C. Williamson, & B. Hatfield. 2014. "Assessing Quality in Toddler Classrooms Using the CLASS-Toddler and the ITERS-R." *Early Education and Development* 25 (6): 875–93.

Lin, V.-K., K. Maxwell, D. Epstein, L. Hutchison, & K. Burgess. 2016. *Data Direction 2: Discussing Data with Families.* Report #2016-32. Bethesda, MD: Child Trends.

Macy, M., & S.J. Bagnato. 2022. "Authentic and Meaningful Developmental Screening in Early Childhood." *Teaching Young Children* 15 (1): 18–21.

McDonald, P. 2018. "Observing, Planning, Guiding: How an Intentional Teacher Meets Standards Through Play." *Young Children* 73 (1): 31–35.

NAEYC. 2020. "Developmentally Appropriate Practice." Position statement. Washington, DC: NAEYC. www.naeyc.org/resources/position-statements/dap.

Peterson, G., & E. Elam. 2020. *Observation and Assessment in Early Childhood Education.* Open Educational Resources Publication by College of the Canyons.

Scott-Little, C. With K. Reschke. 2022. "Foundations of Assessment for Preschool Settings." *Teaching Young Children* 16 (1): 8–11.

About the Author

Rebecca Parlakian is the senior director of programs at ZERO TO THREE. She recently coauthored an early math curriculum, Problem Solvers, for toddlers and preschoolers, as well as a parent education curriculum, Early Connections. Rebecca has also developed a wide range of multimedia resources, including (in partnership with Mount Sinai Parenting Center) the video series, *Sparks*, which highlights the milestones of child development. In addition, she has published articles on topics ranging from dual language development to the impact of screens on very young children. Rebecca holds a master's degree in education and human development, with a concentration in infant-toddler special education, from the George Washington University, where she currently serves as adjunct faculty. Her most important work in child development, however, is her two children, Ella and Bennett.

Unlocking the Potential of Data-Driven Coaching

Child Assessment Evidence as a Guide for Informing Instructional Practices

Christine M. Snyder and Holly P. Delgado

Our memories of being preschoolers often center around baking mud pies and discovering new insects while playing outside, building block towers as high as we could reach, and beginning to understand the magic of reading. But these opportunities to explore, play, and grow didn't just happen. The behind-the-scenes intentional documentation and planning by our teachers set the stage and made that learning come alive. While not readily observable from the perspective of a 4-year-old, teachers' ongoing assessment, reflection, and planning process is an integral component of every high-quality early childhood setting. And yet, like preschoolers' learning environments, teachers' abilities to spark children's learning don't just happen; high-quality, intentional teaching is cultivated with time, effort, and support—ideally, a lot of support.

In this article, we follow two teaching teams—working with the same coach—as they use child assessment data to identify opportunities for the educators to build their knowledge and skills, set meaningful goals, and grow through a supportive coaching process.

> Sam and Lake are preschool coteachers with 25 years of combined teaching experience and have worked as partners in the same classroom for the past eight years. They have had a consistent instructional coach, Jamie, for the past two years and have sought out professional learning opportunities, including training for using their child assessment tool. They stated, "It's helpful to know where children are related to learning. It's how we develop lesson plans, and it guides how we support each child." Because their curriculum model encourages continuity, each teacher has facilitated small group time with the same eight children since the beginning of the school year. When reviewing their assessment data, Sam's reports showed trends high in language and literacy but low in math; Lake's reports showed trends high in math but low in language and literacy.
>
> Kris and Peyton, both relatively new to the field of early childhood education, have been preschool teaching partners for two years. They both maintain positive attitudes toward working with children and in implementing the curriculum. In this first year working with Jamie as their coach, they demonstrated strong adult-child interactions; however, as a teaching team, their child assessment data showed limited growth among the children enrolled in their classroom, and they expressed frustration with the child assessment process, namely that "completing child assessment takes away from interactions with children and actually teaching."

In a supportive environment, the same child assessment data that are used to understand children's growth and progress can also provide valuable insights into teachers' practices. These insights can then be used to create customized coaching plans to enhance instructional activities, strategies, and settings and to promote children's learning.

In our work as coaches and through our examination of research on assessment and coaching, we have found that the key components of a successful coaching process are determining comprehension and motivation and building relationships; setting goals and developing action plans; implementing and individualizing coaching strategies; and tracking progress so as to continuously improve coaching and instruction. In this article, we discuss each coaching process in turn, reviewing general principles and research findings, and we consider implications and examples for our two teaching teams.

Determining Comprehension and Motivation and Building Relationships

As all early childhood educators know, comprehension and motivation are essential for learning. This is just as true for adult learners as it is for children. Thus, one of the first things a coach should consider when developing a coaching relationship is a teacher's levels of comprehension and motivation. The critical question is, "What is the teacher's desired outcome from the coaching relationship?"

Comprehension and Motivation Model

High Comprehension

High Comprehension / High Motivation

- Has a high level of understanding or expertise related to the topic
- Demonstrates an ability to apply knowledge of the topic directly to working with young children
- Seeks additional information and conveys a desire to learn new methods

High Comprehension / Low Motivation

- Has a high level of understanding or expertise related to the topic
- Maintains static teaching practices; operates from the belief, "My teaching practices have worked in the past, so they should still work now"
- Defends the current approach to education and demonstrates a minimal intrinsic desire to learn new methods based on the latest research

High Motivation ⟷ **Low Motivation**

Low Comprehension / High Motivation

- Has limited knowledge related to the topic
- Is eager to learn skills and strategies based on current research; asks questions for clarification
- Seeks support and reassurance; may need assistance to determine how new information can be applied to working with children and families

Low Comprehension / Low Motivation

- Has limited knowledge related to the topic
- Demonstrates indifference to learning new skills; relies on personal preferences rather than research-based teaching strategies
- Meets bare minimum expectations; engages in limited application of information received via professional development

Low Comprehension

Through initial discussions and classroom observations, the coach may want to reflect on the extent to which a teacher seems to comprehend and is motivated to improve on each of the topics—like oral language development, concept of number, and family engagement—that the teacher and coach are planning to work on together. The four-quadrant "Comprehension and Motivation Model" on this page is designed to help coaches think about where each teacher is at the beginning of the coaching process.

As a coach, remember that the characteristics displayed in the "Comprehension and Motivation Model" are not static indicators; teachers differ in comprehension and motivation on each topic. Additionally, individual members of a teaching team may land in different quadrants. Since the goal of coaching is to build individual teacher capacity and improve teaching practices, strategies chosen to support teachers in a coaching relationship should be individualized and designed to convey a partnership approach (WestEd NCSI 2014).

Thinking back to our two teaching teams, Sam and Lake had high comprehension of using data to inform their teaching practices and high motivation to do so to make the children's language, literacy, and mathematics results equally strong. In contrast, although Kris and Peyton had strong adult-child interactions, on the topic of collecting data and using assessment results to inform instruction, they had low comprehension and low motivation.

For Jamie, this points to very different starting places in developing coaching plans. For Kris and Peyton to value the coaching relationship, they need opportunities to see the benefits of taking time to assess the children. They may also need to be shown assessment methods—like taking notes and photos—that are not very time consuming but do offer valuable documentation that can inform instruction.

With an initial understanding of the teachers' comprehension and motivation, the coach is ready to focus on building strong relationships with the teachers. Characteristics of collaborative partnerships include shared understanding of coaching goals, commitment to being supportive, rapport and trust, choice, ongoing communication and support, and celebrations (NCQTL 2015). Goals of coaching should be established up front and created together by the teaching team and the coach.

Support, rapport, and trust can be secured through identifying roles and responsibilities of both the coach and the teachers. Ultimately, coaches strive to "support teachers to see themselves as capable of identifying a problem, collecting and analyzing observational notes and information and making action plans based on what they learn" (Chu 2013, 44). This process is supported through intentional coaching strategies and team reflection. Individuals being coached need to possess a "sincere commitment to change, be able and willing to engage in self-reflection, be willing to engage in collaborative problem-solving process, and be able and willing to try new practices" (Bansal 2012, 15).

When coaching occurs on a regular basis, teachers are more likely to embrace the process with a growth mindset and independently engage in self-guided components of coaching, such as reflection. Coaches need to be able to work with diverse individuals, foster capacity building, maintain professional boundaries, project a timeline, monitor progress, and engage in honest self-reflection about their contributions to the coaching process (Bansal 2012). When coaches take time in the beginning to establish this foundation for a strong, collaborative relationship with clear roles and responsibilities, teachers' commitment to the process tends to increase, as does the likelihood of their success.

> For the two teams, fostering the coaching relationship was equally important but looked different based on each team's needs. For Sam and Lake, it was important that Jamie acknowledge their experience and desire to engage in the growth process. Providing them with strategies they could implement independently was crucial to maintaining their autonomy and confidence.
>
> Kris and Peyton benefited from Jamie starting with their strength—their passion for working with children. Throughout their initial conversations, Jamie acknowledged their hesitation about assessment taking over teaching time and reassured them that teaching would remain their main focus, with assessment-related goals embedded to reduce gaps in child outcomes. Their motivation was centered around their teaching, so it was pivotal for Jamie to integrate that driving factor with motivation to collect and use child assessment data.

Setting Goals and Developing Action Plans

Goal setting is a complex process, especially in the context of coaching. Although designed to improve student outcomes, coaching goals need to be written with a direct focus on improving teaching practices (NCQTL 2015). One widely used rubric for goal development is known by the acronym SMART, which stands for *specific, measurable, assignable, realistic, and time related* (Doran 1981; Haughey 2014). For instructional coaching goals, the SMART concept has been adapted to call for goals that are

- **S**pecific: A distinct skill or child outcome is targeted, and an approach, method, or teaching strategy to be employed is identified
- **M**easurable: Progress can be tracked with concrete evidence
- **A**ssignable: Responsibilities can be delegated to an appropriate member of the teaching team

- **R**ealistic: Resources that are readily available to the teaching team are sufficient
- **T**imely: Results can be achieved within a reasonable time period during the coaching cycle (EL Education 2015)

Using child-level data to inform the SMART goal-setting process, the coach and teachers identify areas of success and opportunities for growth. Guided by the question "What do you want your children to learn?," they comb through the data to identify gaps in evidence (such that progress is not meaningfully being tracked) and opportunities to make more progress in children's learning.

Early childhood educators are directly responsible for both their performances as teachers and the outcomes of children enrolled in their programs. For coaches and teachers to effectively collaborate, they need to regularly analyze individual and group data on children's learning and development and also apply their findings to improve instruction. Together, the coach and teachers should aim for continuous improvement in instructional practices, which means that data collection and analysis must be a continuous and cyclical process (Michigan Department of Education 2016).

Research on coaching has shown that merely having a coach does not guarantee any changes in teachers' practices and thus may not foster improvements in children's learning (O'Keefe 2017). Remaining cognizant of each individual teacher's comprehension and motivation levels on the different topics being addressed in the coaching relationship, an effective coach will facilitate regular, reflective conversations, using data to initiate discussion around child progress and teacher actions. Coaches who ultimately help teachers enhance children's learning ensure that data interpretation remains directly connected to goals, action plans, and the implementation of teaching practices (Michigan Department of Education 2016). Consistent review of data should provide teams with a reflective look at the classroom, allowing teachers the opportunity to carefully evaluate the teaching and learning process. It is important to remember that a regular review of data does not provide answers; rather, it generates questions that help coaching teams determine a direction for future implementation (Trach 2014).

In the initial goal conversation, Sam and Lake quickly identify the noticeable differences the child assessment data revealed in the math and language/literacy domains. Each expressed a desire to promote growth in the areas in which their children had lower scores—for Sam's students, language and literacy; for Lake's small group, math. They shared examples from their respective groups of successful activities and interactions, making notes to later be added to the action plan.

When asked, "What do you want your children to learn?," Peyton and Kris wanted the children to know how to play with others. Upon close examination of the data, Jamie helped them notice that they had the most documentation, particularly anecdotes, in math. Peyton and Kris expressed having an easier time collecting evidence in that area; as Peyton said, "It's easier because I can plan a small group or large group time specific to math." The team discussed strategies for intentional data collection during social interactions, making notes to later add to the action plan.

When data are the focal point of the coaching process, teachers can explore the whys, whats, and hows of the teaching and learning process. Data assist in developing hypotheses about influential factors affecting students' learning (the why), careful consideration of current teaching practices (the what), and decisions regarding changes to curricular implementation and instructional practices (the how) (NAESP 2011). As coaching teams reflect on the whys, whats, and hows, they can begin creating an action plan.

Once goals are established, creating an action plan means identifying concrete steps to be taken to meet the goals by everyone involved in the coaching process. In the action plan, goals should be "prioritized based on the highest need and/or ability to implement change" (Bansal 2012, 15). Intentionally choosing goals with quick and visible results, particularly at the start, may strengthen a teacher's commitment to the coaching process. Collaboratively, the coach and teachers determine a timeline and specific strategies to be implemented and tracked for goal attainment (Bansal 2012). To be as specific as possible in supporting changes in instructional practices, coaching teams consider potential actions and behaviors of children as well as possible adult reactions that are responsive to children and reflective of best teaching practices.

Specific steps in the action plan are strengthened by taking an in-depth look at child-level data and desired outcomes to generate inquiry around effective strategies. Even when the coach and teachers are all very knowledgeable about effective instructional practices, improvement is a messy process. There will be some trial and error, which is why the focus is on a never-ending, cyclical process of gathering and analyzing data and continuous improvement. One very helpful strategy is to refer back to areas of strength, as determined by the data review. Teaching teams ask themselves, "What have been our most effective teaching strategies?" and "How do I apply similar strategies to improve child outcomes in other areas?"

When considering the teaching strategies Sam used to achieve growth in language and literacy scores, Sam shared with Lake, "I began with what children knew and adjusted the materials provided accordingly. For example, to increase alphabetic knowledge, I chose activities in which children manipulated letters—letter cookie cutters, letter stencils, magnetic letters. When children only knew the first letter in their name, I intentionally gave them that particular letter and added other prominent letters in their name."

Likewise, Lake shared strategies that led to increased math outcomes: "I introduced each small group with emphasis on the skill I wanted children to learn. For example, if we were making shape pictures and I wanted children to consider shape attributes as they transform shapes, I might say, 'One day, two triangles were discussing how they were never used to make doors or windows.' I would then start a discussion among the children about shapes and transforming shapes, showing how two triangles together make a square."

Together, Sam and Lake developed lesson plans for their next small group times, taking one another's strategies into consideration.

With Jamie's support, Peyton and Kris discussed strategies for supporting interactions and simultaneously recording anecdotes. In addition to being on the children's level and remaining in proximity to areas where support in social interactions was likely to be needed—such as in the block area—they also decided to make anecdotal note materials available in each area. They hung clipboards with paper and pens in several areas around the classroom and purchased sticky notes and golf pencils to keep in their pockets for use when they are not in the classroom. In order to speed up the note-taking process and to avoid sacrificing interactions with children, Kris and Peyton agreed on acronyms for parts of the daily routine and interest areas, such as "PT" for planning time and "HA" for house area, and they also decided to use children's initials. Jamie shared the strategy "jot to jog," which is jotting down just enough information to jog their memories later when they are inputting their observations into the online assessment platform. Kris and Peyton also considered the use of technology to take photos and to make videos and sound clips, when possible.

When writing lesson plans, Peyton and Kris also started thinking intentionally about assessment. Peyton stated, "We can record the assessment items we think we might observe during our group times." Kris replied, "And we can think about what might happen during work time too. We know the house area will always have pretend play and the book area has a lot of our language and literacy items." Together, Jamie, Kris, and Peyton developed an alignment between their assessment items and the most likely interest areas and times of day in which those items could be assessed.

Action planning provides the road map to goal attainment; it adds intentionality and accountability to the coaching process (NCQTL 2015). It is important to spend time early in the coaching process writing out a detailed action plan—and it is also important to see that plan as a flexible, living document. When the process is revisited regularly and coaching methods are directly tied to teacher motivation and comprehension, teachers achieve greater gains (NCQTL 2015).

Implementing and Individualizing Coaching Strategies

Once the initial action plan has been agreed on by the teachers and coach, implementation begins. A variety of coaching strategies can support teachers' varying levels of comprehension and motivation on the various topics as well as allow for different types of relationships and diverse means of engagement in the growth process.

The following coaching guidelines for visits, strategies, feedback, and reflection, which are based on both the authors' experiences and their review of relevant research, provide concrete and consistent methods for working toward established goals.

Nonnegotiables for Coaching Visits

- Frequent—Coaching visits should be frequent enough to build a relationship and accomplish the goals; what *frequent enough* means should be adjusted based on individual needs of the person(s) being coached (O'Keefe 2017).
- Scheduled—Visits should be planned for days and times that work for all parties involved; this will be unique to each team.

- Limited—Visits should avoid taking on too much at one time; trying to address several aspects of children's learning at once can be overwhelming and reduce efficacy.

Types of Coaching Strategies

- Observing and offering feedback on teachers' strategies for facilitating children's learning
- Visiting other classrooms with strengths in areas of desired growth
- Modeling by coaches or by master teachers
- Receiving in-the-moment guidance from coaches or master teachers
- Reflecting on videos of selected instructional practices (individually and with the team)
- Facilitating small group discussion and reflection
- Engaging in role-playing to practice using new instructional strategies
- Modifying the instructional environment to increase access to materials connected to goals
- Recommending additional professional learning experiences on specific teaching strategies, content areas, and/or assessment tools, as needed

Tips for Delivering Feedback

- Establish ground rules for participation that emphasize continuous improvement.
- Be constructive by describing strategies that are working well and targeting areas for improvement.
- Remain neutral and open-minded; engage in self-reflection to try to be conscious of biases (Bansal 2012).

- Offer specific, objective examples.
- Foster give-and-take throughout the conversation; the coach and teachers should be contributing to the discussion.
- Celebrate successes.
- Review new child assessment data periodically.
- Develop next steps together.

Questions to Initiate and Deepen Reflection

- What did you think about ____?
- What new strategies did you try?
- How does this compare with previous strategies?
- How did that experience feel for you?
- How did children respond?
- What was the impact on children's learning and engagement?
- What new observations of children did you make?
- What would you do the same?
- What would you do differently?
- What do you think would happen if ____?
- How did that compare with ____?
- What additional information do you need?
- What additional support do you need?

After collaborating to develop new instructional activities for each of their small group times, Sam and Lake agreed to have Jamie videotape each of them during facilitation. Later, they watched these videos together, and Jamie facilitated a discussion that reflected on the strategies used.

Sam noted that she had learned from Lake, saying, "Lake, I used your strategy. We pretended we worked in a bake shop and made play dough cookies; then we counted how many chocolate chips (gems) were inside. It was helpful to get the children thinking about counting before I gave them their materials." In watching the video, though, the team also noticed that, although Sam had introduced counting, the focus of small group time quickly turned from math to pretend play. Together, the teachers and their coach discussed strategies that Sam could use to keep the children's focus on counting, such as ordering cookies with a specific number of chocolate chips, asking children to count and compare the number of chocolate chips in their cookies to hers as she worked with them individually, and challenging children to change the quantity by adding or subtracting chocolate chips.

Likewise, while making "alphabet soup" for small group time, Lake had taken Sam's advice and provided children with magnetic letters based on their individual alphabet comprehension. After watching the video and revisiting the anecdotes recorded during this lesson, Lake stated, "I noticed Giovanni wasn't overwhelmed. I only gave him the G in his bowl and although he didn't immediately identify it, he repeated its name and sound and realized they all matched."

Kris and Peyton decided to begin implementation by observing Jamie record anecdotes while she supported social interactions during work time. Later that afternoon, Kris and Peyton sat down with Jamie to discuss their observation of her and to enter Jamie's written anecdotes into their online assessment system. Anecdotes changed from, "WT BA J 1:1-12, said '12 c in my garage'" to "During work time, in the block area, Jackson counted with one-to-one correspondence to 12 and said, '12. There are 12 cars in my garage.'"

While meeting and discussing the observation, the team realized it was possible to both gather assessment evidence and support children's play and interactions. Kris said, "I'm going to need to practice my shorthand, but you [Jamie] didn't spend much time at all actually taking the notes." Peyton agreed: "You made it look so easy. But I can see why it's important that we enter our observations into the online system quickly. I wouldn't remember what those notes meant a few days from now." The next day, the teachers tried out the strategies Jamie had used.

Tracking Progress for Continuous Improvement

From the beginning of a coaching relationship, it is necessary to recognize that coaching is a growth-based, nonlinear process. As part of the process, the coach and teachers should expect to circle back to assessment data to rethink their initial analysis, adjust the coaching plan in response to new data, modify coaching strategies or instructional practices, and adapt successes (if possible) to meet remaining needs. The process should be open and lively, with all parties contributing equally.

To track progress in a way that spurs continuous improvement, coaches and teachers focus on child outcome data and the teachers' progress to discuss the following:

- Did we set the right goals?
- What strategies worked to make progress toward our goals?
- What goals need to be revisited?
- Are there other aspects of children's learning and development that we should examine?
- What are the next steps?

As part of tracking progress and considering revised or new goals, the coach may want to revisit the comprehension and motivation model to determine where members of the teaching teams need additional support.

Using documentation (including videos and anecdotal notes) of small group instruction to guide their reflections, Jamie posed the question, "What strategies worked?" Lake stated, "Individualizing the materials I gave to each child really helped me to scaffold children's learning at their levels." Sam responded, "I can see it helping. My higher-level students engaged more, but my students who are a little lower still did their own thing. It just became play for them. I need more practice introducing my activity and keeping that content focus throughout all of small group time."

Following their own implementation, Kris and Peyton met with Jamie again for reflection. During the feedback conversation, Jamie asked, "What strategies worked?" Kris responded, "Even after one day, I have anecdotes that fill existing gaps in our assessment data, and I was still able to support play. It will take me time to establish anecdotal note taking during play as a consistent habit." Peyton replied, "Yes. It will definitely take time, but I think our assessment app and the use of technology will help us do this too. Instead of writing notes, we can also take a picture and write in the anecdote later."

Each team made a direct connection between the immediate data collection and their new teaching practices to develop next steps and begin the coaching cycle again. Over time, the coaching teams continued to review assessment data to ensure that they made productive changes in their instructional practices and eventually met their goals for supporting children's learning. Just as important for long-term growth, they developed their knowledge and skills related to gathering, analyzing, and acting on child assessment data.

Conclusion

Coaching is a beneficial approach for helping teachers reflect on and improve teaching practices. When coaches and teachers use child assessment data to guide this process, they are able to set goals directly connected to children's learning, improve instructional practices, and track growth over time. As one guide for coaches notes, "The ultimate goal of your work is to increase student achievement and student success. By working to create a data-rich environment, culture and mindset, you will ensure the opportunities for achievement and success for each and every student" (Michigan Department of Education 2016, 70). According to Jamie, "Just like my two teaching teams, when we establish a commitment to improving child outcomes and implement a coaching model for every team, we see increased commitment to the process. Just like scaffolding that happens in the classroom, we see greater results from the coaching process when we meet our teachers at their level. Whether teachers are new to the field, like Kris and Peyton, or seasoned veterans, like Sam and Lake, every teacher has the capacity to grow, learn, and develop alongside the children in their classroom."

Reflection Questions

1. How do you use child assessment data to understand children's growth and development? Do you have a coach or a teaching team to help you unpack and understand the children's growth and learning? How can you foster these relationships?
2. If you do not have a coach or teaching team, how might having one help you as a teacher improve your teaching practices?
3. Looking at the "Comprehension and Motivation Model" on page 58, where do you think you would land on comprehension and on motivation? If you have a coach to support you, how could they help to move you to higher comprehension and higher motivation? If you do not have a coach, what supports in your program could help you?
4. What type of goals would support you in this work? How could you implement your goals and track the progress?

REFERENCES

Bansal, S. 2012. *Effective Coaching in Early Care and Education: Training Manual.* Alameda, CA: First 5 Alameda County. www.first5alameda.org/Documents/ece/Coaching%20Consultation/2012_Coaching_Consultation_FINAL/EffectiveCoachingInEarlyCareAndEducation2012.pdf.

Chu, M. 2013. *Developing Mentoring and Coaching Relationships in Early Care and Education: A Reflective Approach.* Practical Resources in ECE series. London, UK: Pearson Professional Development.

Doran, G.T. 1981. "There's a S.M.A.R.T. Way to Write Management's Goals and Objectives." *Management Review* 70 (11): 35–36.

EL Education. 2015. "Setting Coaching Cycle Goals." Guidance Document. New York: EL Education. https://eleducation.org/resources/setting-coaching-cycle-goals.

Haughey, D. 2014. "A Brief History of Smart Goals." *Project Smart,* December 13. www.projectsmart.co.uk/brief-history-of-smart-goals.php.

Michigan Department of Education. 2016. *Guide to Becoming an Effective Data Coach.* Lansing, MI: Michigan Department of Education.

NAESP (National Association of Elementary School Principals). 2011. *Assessment: Using Student Achievement Data to Support Instructional Decision Making.* White paper. Best Practices for Better Schools series. Alexandria, VA: NAESP. www.naesp.org/sites/default/files/Student_Data_0.pdf.

NCQTL (National Center on Quality Teaching and Learning). 2015. *The Three Components of Practice-Based Coaching: Component 1: Share Goals and Action Planning.* Washington, DC: NCQTL. https://eclkc.ohs.acf.hhs.gov/sites/default/files/pdf/pbc-brief-sgap.pdf.

O'Keefe, B. 2017. *Primetime for Coaching: Improving Instructional Coaching in Early Childhood Education.* Report. Washington, DC: Bellwether Education Partners. https://bellwether.org/publications/primetime-coaching-improving-instructional-coaching-early-childhood-education.

Trach, S.A. 2014. "Inspired Instructional Coaching." *Principal* 92 (2): 12–17.

WestEd NCSI (WestEd National Center for Systemic Improvement). 2014. "Effective Coaching: Improving Teacher Practice and Outcomes for All Learners." Brief. San Francisco: WestEd NCSI. www.air.org/sites/default/files/NCSI_Effective-Coaching-Brief-508.pdf.

About the Authors

Christine M. Snyder, MA, is director of child and family care at University of Michigan, overseeing the campus child care centers and family resources. She has worked in the early childhood education field since 1999 as a teacher, center director, author, and trainer/coach.

Holly P. Delgado, MA, is program director at the University of Michigan Health System Children's Center where she supports infant, toddler, and preschool teachers. With an interest in training and coaching teachers, she maintains a strong focus on high-quality implementation of curriculum and assessment.

Photographs: pp. 56, 61, 63, © Getty Images

Effective Kindergarten Readiness Assessments

Influencing Policy, Informing Instruction, and Creating Joyful Classrooms

Elliot Regenstein, Maia C. Connors, Rio Romero-Jurado, and Joyce Weiner

In the Valley View Community Unit School District, four kindergarten teachers—Stephanie Eick, Patsy Guzman, Shannon Lunardini, and Ashley Volland—have been on the cutting edge of implementing Illinois' kindergarten readiness assessment for the past several years. If you ask them about the impact of the assessment on their classroom practice, they will all give the same answer: it has led to more joy, more play, and more student learning.

Editor's Note

In far too many kindergarten classrooms, teachers feel intense pressure to develop instructional activities that will drive up children's scores on mandated assessments—including, ironically, readiness assessments. With good intentions, but often inadequate knowledge of child development, some leaders have enacted kindergarten assessment and accountability policies that are neither appropriate nor productive. But, as the authors of this article explain, others have done just the opposite. Working with educators, some leaders have found that kindergarten readiness assessments—used regularly, but without high stakes—can support joyful, playful learning and inform state-level decision making (such as which communities should receive additional resources).

Teachers who cultivate joyful learning honor both the fundamentals of early childhood and the need to further children's growth and development. That means building on children's interests, providing time for exploration, and engaging with children's stories and dramatic play (and more!). It also means deeply understanding the content areas, closely observing children's current knowledge and abilities, and carefully planning appropriately challenging learning environments and activities.

To be responsive to children's needs, teachers must frequently and systematically collect information on children's growing knowledge, skills, and interests across academic, social, and emotional domains. It's a daunting task. But as this article shows, policymakers and administrators can help by providing well-informed, flexible guidelines on kindergarten readiness assessments. Used as snapshots of current abilities (not as tools for accountability), these assessments help teachers design lessons, centers, and projects that are engaging, meaningful, and joyful for every child.

As assessment becomes more common in early childhood, teachers, administrators, and policymakers should work together. This article on sensible, supportive, flexible uses of kindergarten readiness assessments can provide a model and will hopefully spur needed discussions.

—Lisa Hansel, former editor in chief of *Young Children*

Across the country, state policymakers and district leaders are increasingly seeking to implement kindergarten readiness assessments because they provide valuable information about the skills that children bring with them when they enter school. Used wisely, they help teachers, schools, districts, and states understand how to better support children's development. Ideally, every school district would experience these new assessments as useful tools that inform instruction. The key lesson learned in Valley View's implementation is important: teachers need time and support to get adjusted to kindergarten readiness assessment practice—and if they have that time and support, they can use the assessment results to create rich, engaging learning environments that are well matched to children's needs and interests.

As early childhood education policy analysts and researchers, we have analyzed the use of kindergarten readiness assessment results throughout the United States and the potential impacts of using those results for improper purposes. Our paper, *Uses and Misuses of Kindergarten Readiness Assessment Results* (Regenstein et al. 2017), offers a detailed analysis of why some uses of kindergarten readiness assessment results are appropriate and others are not (see "Improving Practice" on page 70). Here, we discuss the most essential issues surrounding classroom- and school-level uses of these assessments, drawing on both our paper and our informative interviews with the kindergarten teachers in Valley View.

Improving Practice

As early learning systems have grown and matured, there has been an increase in the use of kindergarten readiness assessments (KRAs) that measure where children are developmentally as they transition into kindergarten. Kindergarten readiness assessments have been a valuable tool for leaders and practitioners to identify gaps in children's knowledge and skills and to enhance teaching and learning.

Within the broad category of improving practice, there are numerous specific efforts that KRAs can support:

- KRA results can be used to develop "ready schools"—that is, schools that are well-designed to meet the needs of their incoming kindergartners. Using KRAs in a school can inform a community conversation about the needs of the incoming kindergarten cohort, which can inform early learning program design and transition planning for children and families.
- KRAs can support early learning and kindergarten classrooms in aligning their practices by informing teachers about the overall strengths and weaknesses of each cohort's skills at kindergarten entry, in order to better target instruction and strengthen transitions.
- KRAs can also support teachers' understanding of children's learning and advance their knowledge of child development as they document each child's knowledge and competencies and identify a child's strengths and areas in need of improvement.
- KRAs can also foster teacher-parent partnerships. Families can be included as part of the process of sharing what they know about their child's learning and also given information about their child's development that can support learning needs at home.
- KRAs can provide useful information—along with results from screenings and other observations—to identify children who should be referred for evaluation of potential developmental delays or other special needs.

Successfully implementing KRAs for any instructional purpose requires ongoing training and supports for teachers conducting the assessment; teachers administering the assessment should not only be trained on the tool(s) being used but also knowledgeable in child development, children's capabilities and cultural and linguistic backgrounds, and guiding principles for assessment. Teachers also need training in how to use assessment data in order to make decisions and plan activities to support child improvement. Conducting ongoing cycles of assessment to inform instruction is time consuming for teachers and resource intensive for schools, and it demands that school leaders protect the time necessary to do the work correctly if the results are to be meaningful. Thus, an intentional investment and recognition of the benefits by administrators and teachers are imperative for meaningful formative use of KRAs to improve instruction.

Ensuring Equity in Kindergarten Readiness Assessments

Developing and implementing a kindergarten readiness assessment that accurately assesses young children coming from culturally, linguistically, and ethnically diverse backgrounds is critical considering the value of KRAs in guiding practice, identifying an individual child's abilities and needs, and informing policies and resource decision-making. Given the limited number of assessment instruments that have been designed or adapted with these populations in mind, experts have noted important considerations and challenges to ensuring validity and reliability in assessments. For example, young dual-language learners may be assessed in multiple languages, which raises issues around assessment availability in other languages and the cultural familiarity and language skills of the assessor. Assessors need to be fluent in both English and the preferred or dominant language of the child and have appropriate versions of the same assessment to be able to administer the assessment effectively. Moreover, assessors need training on the indicators of typical language development for children speaking another language and guidance on how best to report and interpret such results from multiple languages, and they must be knowledgeable about the children's cultural and community contexts. These considerations, along with others experts have identified, must continue to be explored and addressed to ensure valid findings and well-guided policy decisions that are equitable and truly benefit young children.

> Excerpted from E. Regenstein, M. Connors, R. Romero-Jurado, & J. Weiner, *Uses and Misuses of Kindergarten Readiness Assessment Results* (Policy Conversations No. 6, 2017).
>
> This excerpt offers a small sample of the full report, which is available for free online. For a more detailed look at the benefits of kindergarten readiness assessments, an important discussion of why these assessments should not be used to make high-stakes decisions, and extensive references, go to www.startearly.org/app/uploads/pdf/PolicyConversationKRA2017.pdf.

What Is Kindergarten Readiness?

For educators to assess kindergarten readiness, it has to be defined. Fortunately, in most states there is a formalized operating definition of kindergarten readiness (Connors-Tadros 2013; Regenstein et al. 2017). While those definitions vary, there are a few characteristics that are common across states:

- Readiness encompasses multiple domains of growth and development. State early learning standards generally take this into account by addressing a wide range of domains (Early Childhood Education Research Alliance 2013; Education Commission of the States 2014; Regenstein et al. 2017). The exact names of domains may vary, but they generally include concepts like language and literacy, cognition, general knowledge (including early science and mathematics concepts), approaches to learning, physical well-being and motor development, and social and emotional development (Regenstein et al. 2017; Shepard, Kagan, & Wertz 1998).
- Young learners develop skills and abilities across all of these developmental domains in a highly interrelated manner, building confidence and expertise as new competencies are mastered. But children often progress unevenly within and across domains, meaning that ongoing observations may be needed to get a sense of a child's developmental trajectory (Regenstein et al. 2017; Snow 2011).
- Similarly, there is high variability in what is considered the "normal range" of child development (Meisels 2006; NAEYC 2009). Young children are constantly developing and acquiring new skills, but the rate at which early learners acquire new concepts and skills varies significantly among children.

Although some states do not have a formal definition of kindergarten readiness, they all have a de facto definition of kindergarten readiness in their learning standards. That is, all 50 states have learning standards that cover the pre-kindergarten years and are articulated to some degree by standards for kindergarten (Education Commission of the States 2014; Regenstein et al. 2017). These learning standards from both early learning and K–12 provide a guide to educators about what kindergarten readiness should look like.

Once kindergarten readiness has been defined, it can be measured. And in the Valley View district—where the assessment is implemented well and the results are used to enhance the learning environment—that is where the fun begins. Neither teachers nor children feel pressure; in fact, teachers find that the assessment helps them identify children's interests and craft activities that help children grow.

How Assessments Contribute to Joyful Learning

While most educators probably do not equate kindergarten readiness assessments with increasing the joy in learning, they can be excellent tools for just that. These tips will help teachers and administrators maximize the benefits of their assessments:

- Use kindergarten readiness assessments to get to know the children better—not just their needs as learners, but also their emerging and long-term interests.
- Implement the assessments as a natural part of teachers' interactions with children; this will prevent children from feeling pressure and give teachers a more accurate picture of current strengths, needs, and opportunities.
- Engage a wide range of colleagues in the assessment process in order to more deeply understand each child. Also engage those colleagues in creating new, interdisciplinary learning opportunities for each child.
- Use frequent assessments as an opportunity to engage in new creative activities or try out innovative learning centers; the assessment results will help gauge the effectiveness of the new approaches and support reflection and refinement over time.
- Avoid misusing assessment results; while kindergarten readiness assessments inform instruction, they should not be used for high-stakes accountability (for children, teachers, or schools).

Assessing Kindergarten Readiness

"Students don't realize they're being assessed in any way," says Ms. Volland. Assessment tools will generally ask teachers to evaluate children in multiple domains. An initial assessment will occur in the fall as children begin their kindergarten year, and the best tools call for additional evaluations throughout the school year. While each of the four Valley View kindergarten teachers uses some different approaches, a few common themes have emerged. These include

- Assessing children during center time, rather than one on one, because it feels more natural to the children.
- Inquiring about the children's activities. The teachers approach children who are already working on something and start asking questions about it. As Ms. Guzman says, they are "learning while they are playing." She adds that she will ask them questions about what they are doing that build on their areas of interest.
- Using technology, such as a tablet, to record answers and take photos of what they are seeing in their classroom. One teacher also uses an app to organize the evidence by domain.
- Soliciting feedback from gym teachers, librarians, and music and art teachers to get a richer sense of how the children are developing.

At Valley View, the teachers expressed enthusiasm for the assessment tool they use—the Kindergarten Individual Development Survey (KIDS) (ISBE, n.d.). The teachers discussed ways that KIDS helped them understand the strengths and needs of their children, which in turn allowed them to develop activities that added joy to the classroom. It also strengthened collaboration among teachers—when a strategy for ramping up the fun was a hit in one classroom, it quickly spread to others.

Across the country, there is a wide range of assessment tools in use, and consensus is still emerging on the state of the art in kindergarten readiness assessment. The National Research Council has recommended some best practices for assessment tools—including that they should be used by teachers in the classroom environment throughout the kindergarten year, collect information on multiple domains of development, and be valid and reliable (Snow & Van Hemel 2008). In particular, it is important that assessments support equity—they must be designed to account for culturally, linguistically, and ethnically diverse backgrounds (Regenstein et al. 2017).

Even though there are many different kindergarten readiness assessment tools, there are two basic categories of uses for the results of those assessments: (1) improving practice at the school level and (2) analyzing system-wide needs at the policy level. Both are briefly discussed in the following sections.

Using Kindergarten Readiness Assessment Results to Improve Practice

"Data help us differentiate and give specific kids the help they need to progress," Ms. Lunardini says, adding that data also provide useful information to specialists at the school. Some of the specific benefits the teachers identified include

- Improving their ability to form successful groups within the classroom
- Helping to identify interventions that might be beneficial to specific children, such as targeted instruction or a speech therapist
- Gaining a better understanding of the social and emotional needs of their children; as Ms. Volland says, the assessment has helped her "get to know each student on a deeper level," and Ms. Guzman adds that it has "broadened my way of looking at students"
- Understanding children's interests and preferences, including which children need more time to think before contributing to a discussion and which ones benefit from more hands-on activities

Because the assessment required teachers to consider their students' problem-solving skills and ability to work together, the teachers universally reported that they were doing more to support those skills and abilities in the classroom—and that it was paying off. They reported that children were taking more initiative to solve problems among themselves, and were learning more independently. One teacher even reported that sometimes when a student was asking her a question, another student would jump in to help answer.

A more challenging area for the teachers was communicating results to parents. The teachers acknowledged the tricky balance of giving parents more specific, child-centered information than they were receiving before without overwhelming them with too much data. While the teachers have had the benefit of training in how to analyze the data, parents have not. The teachers thought the reports produced from their assessment were potentially too dense for parents to understand easily, and teachers' individual efforts to work around that challenge have not been consistently successful. Moreover, the teachers found that some parents were expecting feedback from teachers to be focused on what the parents think of as "academic" development, but the teachers thought it was important to discuss with parents their newfound perspective on the children's growing social and emotional skills. To improve communication with parents, Illinois recently developed a website (www.isbe.net/kids) with more information on the assessment.

System-Wide Measurement of Kindergarten Readiness

States are increasingly looking to use kindergarten readiness assessments as a system-wide measurement of children's strengths and needs when they enter kindergarten. Maryland has been a pioneer in this area, using data from kindergarten readiness assessments to help inform early learning investments (Regenstein et al. 2017). Because it is so difficult for schools to help students catch up when they fall behind grade-level expectations, schools, districts, and states should use these assessment results to proactively address the common challenges found within groups of incoming kindergartners (Regenstein et al. 2017).

As valuable as this information can be, it is important that the results of kindergarten readiness assessments not be misused. Some potential *misuses* of the information include the following:

- Using individual kindergarten readiness scores to hold a child back or prevent a child from enrolling in kindergarten
- Holding individual early learning programs accountable for the results their former students produce on kindergarten readiness assessments
- Measuring the quality of teaching, or holding teachers accountable for the kindergarten readiness of their students

No existing kindergarten readiness assessments were designed for any of these purposes—and for the latter two in particular, there are a host of measurement challenges that make using the assessment results unreliable and inappropriate for those purposes (Regenstein et al. 2017). There are important differences between kindergarten readiness assessments and the accountability assessments that begin in third grade, so just because they are all called "assessments" does not mean that they can all be used in the same ways. Simply put, the kindergarten readiness assessments currently available cannot be used for accountability purposes.

Supporting Effective Implementation

"Everyone has to participate in the training process," Ms. Eick says. For administrators and teachers in Valley View, maximizing the benefits of their assessment is an ongoing effort that has already been in effect several years. The Valley View teachers have learned some important lessons that can make the assessment process more joyful and effective in other districts as well:

- Take it one step at a time. Ms. Lunardini noted that her team worked on literacy the first year, then math the next. That approach provided time to master the different elements of the assessment.

- Do not expect to get everything right the first time. Ms. Volland noted that she had tried various ways of keeping data; it took her many iterations to come up with a system she really felt comfortable with. She has shared her tools with other teachers to help them speed up the process, but she knows that all teachers have to figure out what works for them.
- Work together. Ms. Guzman emphasized that partnership and mentorship among teachers are essential.

While teachers can do a lot to help each other, they also need leadership and support from administrators. Many principals have limited experience with the development of young children; according to a survey by the National Association of Elementary School Principals, most principals who are early in their careers feel like they could improve their understanding of child development (Education Week 2015; Loewenberg 2015). Indeed, if principals come to the job primarily with experience teaching older children, they might not know what great kindergarten instruction really looks like (Szekely 2013). In particular, they may not appreciate the importance of creating a joyful learning environment, including building on children's interests through centers, guided play, and free play.

The Valley View teachers noted that implementing KIDS helps their administrators really understand what it means for teachers to do great work with young children. One principal provided supplies like play kitchens and tool sets to support play in the classroom; another even said "A noisy classroom is a learning classroom" because children should be talking with each other. Ms. Eick explained that principals were increasingly understanding that play can include purposeful play-based learning in curricular activities aligned with the standards, and that it is a false dichotomy to talk about learning and play as two separate things (Hassinger-Das, Hirsh-Pasek, & Golinkoff 2017).

Beyond training on child development, successfully implementing kindergarten readiness assessments for any instructional purpose requires ongoing training and support for teachers conducting the assessment. To be effective, teachers need to be trained on how to administer the tool and on how to then use the data to support children's learning and development (Guss et al. 2015). Conducting ongoing cycles of assessment to inform instruction requires a meaningful investment of time and resources. The payoff can be worth it, but for the results to be useful, school leaders and teachers must protect the time necessary to do this work carefully and completely.

All of the Valley View teachers acknowledged that it had taken them several years to master the assessment process. The Valley View teachers agreed that the perspective of teachers who have been through the process before can be useful to those just starting out. In schools that are trying these kinds of assessments for the first time, bringing in some of those experienced voices could be very useful. In schools where assessments are already up and running, experienced teachers should be given time to mentor the newer teachers.

Conclusion

For Valley View's teachers, kindergarten readiness has changed how they do business. It is "not a shift away from rigorous instruction, but a different way of providing it," as Ms. Eick puts it. These four teachers and their colleagues are leveraging assessment to create a more joyful classroom by learning how to better observe their students, collecting information about how their students are learning, and then using that information to inform instruction. Because kindergartners love to learn, good kindergarten readiness assessments will help teachers understand children's strengths and challenges as well as keep up with their natural curiosity and respond to their social and emotional needs.

Moreover, the experiences of teachers and principals with kindergarten readiness assessment should help inform policy choices that increase support for the education of young children, in kindergarten and earlier. Kindergarten classrooms benefit not only from teachers who understand how to help their students but also from children who come into them ready for what's ahead. Stronger investments in preschool and infant-toddler programs can give more children the educational opportunities they need.

Kindergarten readiness assessments can be a valuable resource for creating joyful classrooms where children's needs are met and interests are pursued. For these four Valley View teachers, the journey has been well worth it. With the right tools and supports, it can be worth it for many more teachers in schools around the country.

Reflection Questions

1. Think about how you use various assessments in your classroom, including your school or district's kindergarten readiness assessment. Were the assessments developed for these purposes? Are the different assessments you use aligned with each other? How are the results being used and communicated?
2. What does an appropriate assessment for kindergarten readiness look like? What types of kindergarten readiness assessments would provide data to improve children's success in kindergarten?
3. How else do you assess growth, development, and learning through play in your classroom? How do you collect data and document it?

REFERENCES

Connors-Tadros, L. 2013. "Overview of State Kindergarten Readiness Definitions." Center on Enhancing Early Learning Outcomes (CEELO) presentation to the Arkansas Kindergarten Readiness Indicators Committee, in Little Rock, Arkansas. http://ceelo.org/resources/overview-of-state-kindergarten-readiness-definitions.

Early Childhood Education Research Alliance. 2013. "Implementing Early Learning Standards: Lessons from Research and Practice." Bridge webinar presented by Regional Educational Laboratory Northeast and Islands (REL-NEI) and Center on Enhancing Early Learning Outcomes (CEELO), April 14. www.ctearlychildhood.org/uploads/6/3/3/7/6337139/ecea-4-24-13-bridge-webinar.pdf.

Education Commission of the States. 2014. "50-State Comparison: Kindergarten Standards—General Info." http://ecs.force.com/mbdata/mbquestRT?rep=Kq1410.

Education Week. 2015. "New Principals: A Data Snapshot." *Education Week* 35 (1): 6. www.edweek.org/ew/section/multimedia/new-principals-a-data-snapshot.html.

Guss, S.S., M. Sweet-Darter, B. Mangus, & A. Stein. 2015. *Measuring Data Utilization: A Report Examining Data Utilization Applicable to Educare Schools*. Literature review. www.educareschools.org/educare-schools-improving-programs-use-data.

Hassinger-Das, B., K. Hirsh-Pasek, & R.M. Golinkoff. 2017. "The Case of Brain Science and Guided Play: The Developing Story." *Young Children* 72 (2): 45–49.

ISBE (Illinois State Board of Education). n.d. "KIDS: Every Illinois Child Ready for Kindergarten." Early Childhood Division. www.isbe.net/kids.

Loewenberg, A. 2015. "Many New Principals Lack Early Ed Knowledge." Education Policy. New America. www.newamerica.org/education-policy/edcentral/elem-principals-prek.

Meisels, S.J. 2006. "Accountability in Early Childhood: No Easy Answers." Occasional Paper 6. Herr Research Center for Children and Social Policy, Erikson Institute.

NAEYC. 2009. "Developmentally Appropriate Practice in Early Childhood Programs Serving Children from Birth through Age 8." Position statement. Washington, DC: NAEYC. www.naeyc.org/files/naeyc/file/positions/PSDAP.pdf.

Regenstein, E., M. Connors, R. Romero-Jurado, & J. Weiner. 2017. *Uses and Misuses of Kindergarten Readiness Assessment Results*. Policy Conversations No. 6. Chicago: The Ounce of Prevention Fund. www.startearly.org/app/uploads/2020/09/PUBLICATION_Uses-and-Misuses-of-Kindergarten-Readiness-Assessment-Results.pdf.

Shepard, L., S.L. Kagan, and E. Wertz, eds. 1998. *Principles and Recommendations for Early Childhood Assessments*. Washington, DC: National Education Goals Panel. https://govinfo.library.unt.edu/negp/reports/prinrec.pdf.

Snow, C.E., & S.B. Van Hemel, eds. 2008. *Early Childhood Assessment: Why, What, and How*. Report of the National Research Council. Washington, DC: National Academies Press. www.nap.edu/catalog/12446/early-childhood-assessment-why-what-and-how.

Snow, K. 2011. *Developing Kindergarten Readiness and Other Large-Scale Assessment Systems: Necessary Considerations in the Assessment of Young Children*. Washington, DC: NAEYC Center for Applied Research.

Szekely, A. 2013. "Leading for Early Success: Building School Principals' Capacity to Lead High-Quality Early Education." Washington, DC: National Governors Association. www.nga.org/files/live/sites/NGA/files/pdf/2013/1306LeadingForEarlySuccessPaper.pdf.

About the Authors

Elliot Regenstein is a partner at Foresight Law + Policy. He was formerly the senior vice president for advocacy and policy at the Ounce of Prevention Fund (now Start Early).

Maia C. Connors, PhD, is research associate professor and executive director of the Early Childhood Research Alliance of Chicago at the Institute for Policy Research at Northwestern University. She was formerly the director of research and policy initiatives at Start Early.

Rio Romero-Jurado, MA, is assistant director of national policy at Start Early. Rio supports the Educare Learning Network's collective policy and advocacy efforts and Start Early's work to advance equitable early childhood policy and systems.

Joyce Weiner was senior policy manager with both the Illinois and national policy teams at Start Early, where she developed state systems and policies leading to a well-prepared, diverse early childhood (birth to 8 years) workforce.

Photographs and Learning Progressions

Supports for Intentional Assessment and Instruction in Mathematics

Sarah Roller Dyess, Elizabeth Petit Cunningham, and Katherine Ariemma Marin

Alex is playing with the wooden blocks during free choice time. At first glance, Mr. Webb sees Alex's construction as another tower or building, not an uncommon sight in his kindergarten classroom. But on further inspection, Mr. Webb notices Alex's careful attention to symmetry, indicating her ability to compose and decompose 3-D shapes.

Mr. Webb wants to capture Alex's mathematical thinking to share with his colleagues. They will soon begin planning a unit on geometry using learning trajectories, and he thinks Alex's elaborate building would be an excellent example for the group to discuss. He quickly grabs his tablet and snaps a photo of the structure while he asks Alex to tell him a little bit about it. Alex tells Mr. Webb, "I used the rectangle blocks, and I put them here and here. And I put triangles here and here to build the towers for the castle."

Mr. Webb brings the photo, along with other photos of children's block play, to the team planning meeting. He uses the photos to display some of the children's background knowledge and current experiences connected to composing and decomposing shapes. The teachers look at the learning trajectory for composition of 3-D shapes, and together they figure out how the photos span the learning progression.

Based on their new understanding, the teachers select activities that will continue to advance children's learning about geometry through experiences with building blocks and other materials.

Collecting evidence from observation and then using it to plan instruction is challenging work, particularly in preschool and early primary grades. Children frequently showcase their mathematical thinking using materials that will be moved around during learning and put away at the end of math activities, leaving their mathematical thinking undocumented. Teachers often use observation tools or checklists to record evidence of children's thinking (Fennell, Kobett, & Wray 2017). Using these types of tools requires teachers to skillfully attend to and interpret a child's work and talk, often in a moment filled with the buzz of a classroom full of young children (Jacobs et al. 2011).

Photograph capturing Alex's understanding of composing and decomposing shapes.

One way to simplify teachers' work of attending to and interpreting children's thinking is to give teachers more time to analyze evidence. Capturing children's thinking using photographs enables teachers to examine children's work later on, when they have time to reflect on *what* children know and *how* children understand it. Furthermore, the photographs can be an effective starting point for the formative assessment cycle focused on *assessment for learning* (Wiliam 2017), which can be informed by learning progressions (Ebby & Petit 2018).

This article describes how two tools—photographs and learning trajectories—can be used to capture children's mathematical thinking and reflect on it to make instructional decisions as part of the formative assessment process. To illustrate this, we consider the case of Ms. Lopez, a preservice teacher, as she uses these tools to document and make sense of children's additive reasoning in a kindergarten math station.

Capturing Children's Mathematical Thinking with Photographs

Documenting children's understanding is a key element of formative assessment, and when it comes to mathematical thinking, the use of photographs offers many benefits. Photographs can give teachers and families visual evidence of children's mathematical development over time (Krechevsky et al. 2013). In preschool and primary classrooms, the mathematical work of children is not always expressed in a written form; photographs capture children's math activities with blocks, counters, games, and other materials (Tapper 2012). In addition, photographs provide teachers with evidence of children's understandings that can be analyzed at a later time, away from the buzz of the classroom (Sherin & van Es 2003). The use of photographs makes it possible for teachers to make sense of children's mathematical thinking outside of the classroom moment and to plan future math instruction more intentionally.

Understanding Children's Progress with Learning Trajectories

Learning trajectories (Clements & Sarama 2014), or learning progressions (Ebby & Petit 2018), have been created to synthesize and reflect research and knowledge about how children learn and understand mathematics. Learning progressions provide teachers with a framework for interpreting children's mathematical thinking and can be used when planning instruction to move children's understandings forward (Ebby & Petit 2018). For example, the Ongoing Assessment Project (OGAP) Additive Framework displays the strategies children may use when counting and solving additive problems (OGAP Math LLC 2017). It also provides illustrations of student work that teachers can expect to see when children solve additive problems, beginning with counting strategies and moving toward more complex and generalizable strategies. Having an image of what children's thinking might look like when they are working supports teachers so they can (1) plan by anticipating children's strategies and responses to a problem or task; (2) be prepared to carefully observe children so that their mathematical thinking and strategies are easier to identify and capture in the moment; (3) interpret children's work; and (4) design instruction that builds on children's current understandings and moves their mathematical thinking forward.

More About Learning Trajectories

To deepen your understanding of learning trajectories and find sample activities, games, and other useful classroom tools, check out these free online resources:

- Ongoing Assessment Project (OGAP), Resources and Related Publications—https://ogapmathllc.com/resources-and-related-publications/#151-ogap-frameworks
- "Formative Assessment Tools to Improve Early Math Learning"—https://stemforall2018.videohall.com/presentations/1186
- Learning and Teaching with Learning Trajectories [LT]^2—www.learningtrajectories.org

Ms. Lopez's Math Station

Ms. Lopez, the preservice teacher, is taking an elementary mathematics methods course taught by the first author. An assignment in the instructional methods course is to create a math station (Diller 2011) for use as a formative assessment tool. The assignment asks preservice teachers to engage children in the math station, photograph evidence of the children's mathematical thinking at the station, analyze the photographs, and consider potential next instructional steps based on those analyses. Ms. Lopez decided to complete the assignment in her field placement, a kindergarten classroom where she had been observing the teacher and the children.

Ms. Lopez knew the children had been working on counting from 0 to 20, so she created her math station to extend the children's mathematical experiences by meeting two instructional goals: (1) to identify a number from 0 to 20 and then build the numbers that are one more and one less than the original number, and (2) to practice writing numbers from 0 to 20 that represent a set of objects. In the math station, the children each selected a number from a deck of number cards and used apple-shaped erasers to create concrete representations of their numbers. Then the children determined which numbers were one more and one less and represented those values with erasers. Finally, on a recording sheet, the children wrote the numbers.

Before engaging children at the math station, Ms. Lopez spent time examining the OGAP Additive Framework to familiarize herself with the ways children might represent and count the selected quantities. Reviewing the framework helped her determine that the key objective of her formative assessments (and the photographs) would be to notice and document how children were counting. Specifically, she wanted to know if and how children organized or grouped the concrete objects. Ms. Lopez thought photographing this aspect of the children's activities at the station was appropriate because once children left the math station, the concrete objects would be put away and the evidence of their thinking would no longer be available to inform her instructional planning.

Photograph showing two children's placement of counters, with Rosa (left) beginning to count by fours while Jillian (right) counts by ones.

Once all of the children completed the math station activity, Ms. Lopez looked at the photographs she had taken during the activity and selected a few to use for the course assignment. Here, we examine two of the photographs Ms. Lopez selected and discuss how each increased her understanding of the children's mathematical thinking.

Ms. Lopez described the photograph on page 81 as follows: "[The photograph] provided an accurate representation of [how] two children chose to solve their number card using different strategies." Examining the photo, which was taken mid-activity, she noted that Rosa (the student on the left) had begun organizing the apples by creating rows of four, whereas Jillian (the student on the right) was counting her apples by ones and had them all together in a single group. According to Ms. Lopez, Rosa's organizational strategy was based on her previous knowledge: "Rosa preferred placing her counters in groups of four because she felt confident in her ability to count by fours. Rosa said her counting strategy reminded her of counting quarters. She knew that four quarters make a dollar, and that's how she wanted to count."

Rosa then used her organizational strategy to help Jillian. "Rosa explained to Jillian how she could group her counters into groups of five to help make her counting easier," Ms. Lopez recalled. From her observation, Ms. Lopez noticed something else: "Jillian felt confident in her ability to count groups of fives, and this made it easier for her to identify one more and one less."

The second photograph Ms. Lopez described (on this page) considered the strategy of skip counting but highlighted a student misconception. She wrote,

> I selected this photo because this shows that Shannon was trying to figure out a way she could place her counters so it would be easier for her to count. Shannon attempted to count by twos and she did so in an unexpected way. She was not counting like 2, 4, 6, 8, etc.; instead, Shannon was saying 2 + 2 + 2 + 2 + 2 = 10. Shannon was struggling to keep track of how many times she added two plus two plus two.

Photograph showing Shannon learning to count by twos.

Ms. Lopez's analyses of the photographs demonstrate her ability to attend to the mathematics in the photographs. Her analyses also highlight the power of having photographs to capture children's thinking—including photographs of in-progress activities that show children's thinking as it is happening rather than "finished products"—and to allow time for in-depth analyses later. Using her photographs, Ms. Lopez was able to specifically describe the strategies the children were using, whether grouping by fours or fives or counting by ones, and she was able to recognize the challenges Shannon experienced when trying to add twos. She was also able to describe and interpret the children's strategies. She acknowledged that Rosa had an efficient strategy for counting while Jillian did not, and that Rosa's strategy was illustrative and enabled the children to work together to advance Jillian's counting strategies. Ms. Lopez's use of photographs to capture and interpret children's mathematical thinking and actions provided her with formative assessment data she could use to plan for further student learning.

After Ms. Lopez made sense of the children's thinking that was visible in all of the photographs she took throughout the activity, she used the OGAP Additive Framework as a way of identifying and describing the children's understandings, based on the images in the framework's learning progressions. For example, Ms. Lopez stated, "Rosa's strategy falls under the flexible counting section of the OGAP Framework because there is evidence of her counting by twos, fours, and fives, as well as identifying one more and one less."

In the moment, while Rosa was engaged at the math station, Ms. Lopez had many responsibilities in the classroom. It would have been nearly impossible for her to spend the time or give the attention necessary to Rosa's work in order to analyze it and determine where it belonged in the learning progressions. Taking photographs gave her the ability to analyze Rosa's strategies thoroughly and accurately when she had more time.

Ms. Lopez also used the OGAP Additive Framework to figure out her next instructional steps. For example, she began by describing how Shannon's counting strategy of adding 2 + 2 + 2 + 2 + 2 was evidence that Shannon's work would be considered an early counting strategy. She went on to suggest the following instructional steps:

> Shannon needs extra help to construct meaning of numbers and to better make sense of numbers. Shannon would benefit from working with the teacher one-on-one to build her counting fluency. Once Shannon was able to visually see her counters, she was able to identify one more and one less, with the help of her partner.

Using the OGAP Additive Framework to identify Shannon's work along a developmental progression of additive reasoning, Ms. Lopez was able to suggest the instructional next step of "working with the teacher one-on-one to build her counting fluency." Although this is not a sophisticated instructional suggestion, it is a thoughtful beginning step for a preservice teacher and a step that was made possible by the opportunity to examine the child's thinking outside of the moment.

Another benefit of photographs is that they enable meaningful collaboration with colleagues outside the classroom. Ms. Lopez's instructional methods professor challenged her thinking about how she could better connect the evidence in Shannon's work to a more productive instructional response. Together, they used the photograph and the OGAP Additive Framework to construct an alternative plan for next instructional steps. In those next steps, they leveraged Shannon's desire to use skip counting as a strategy and gave her concrete models to explore and practice skip counting.

The important idea to consider in this case is that planning for and collecting photographic evidence, coupled with the use of learning progressions, enabled Ms. Lopez to identify children's mathematical thinking, make sense of it, label it along a developmental trajectory, and consider instructional next steps, all of which are key elements of the formative assessment cycle.

Conclusion

This case illustrates how teachers can use photographs and learning trajectories as tools to support formative assessment practices and intentional instruction. The photographs provide a means of capturing evidence of children's mathematical thinking that would otherwise have disappeared following the math activity. The visual structures of various additive strategies in the OGAP Additive Framework offer the teacher a lens through which to notice and identify important mathematical thinking to capture in photographs. Analyses of the photographs with the learning progressions further support the teacher as she interprets the thinking children are doing and identifies how to build on their thinking for future instruction. In this way, photographs serve as a vehicle for the formative assessment cycle.

Reflection Questions

1. Mathematical thinking and learning happen everywhere, not just during intentional math learning experiences. Think about opportunities and experiences in your classroom where children demonstrate mathematical thinking that you can photograph to document and reflect on their learning. (For example, in the opening vignette of this article, Mr. Webb captured Alex's block play during free choice time, which indicated her thinking about symmetry and composing and decomposing shapes.)
2. How could you create or improve on a math station in your classroom? Based on the mathematical concept or unit being focused on, what types of materials would you include in the station? What activities would you photograph to document and monitor children's learning progressions?
3. Who could you collaborate with to discuss photographs and other documentation to help support your own teaching and reflective practice? How would this help inform your curriculum and instruction practices?

We invite teachers to plan photographic opportunities in their classrooms and to try using photographs along with learning progressions as a way to capture and make meaning of formative assessment data that typically disappear during cleanup time. Similar to Ms. Lopez, we encourage teachers to select a few photographs to investigate in more detail. The following questions might be used to guide this investigation:

- What evidence of mathematical thinking is present in your photographs?
- Are any of the strategies children used identifiable in the learning progressions?
- What strategies do I want to encourage or build on in tomorrow's instruction?

REFERENCES

Clements, D.H., & J. Sarama. 2014. *Learning and Teaching Early Math: The Learning Trajectories Approach.* 2nd ed. Studies in Mathematical Thinking and Learning series. New York: Routledge.

Diller, D. 2011. *Math Work Stations: Independent Learning You Can Count On, K–2.* Portland, ME: Stenhouse; Markham, ONT: Pembroke.

Ebby, C., & M.M. Petit. 2018. "Using Learning Trajectories to Elicit, Interpret, and Respond to Student Thinking." In *A Fresh Look at Formative Assessment in Mathematics Teaching*, eds. E.A. Silver & V.L. Mills, 81–102. Reston, VA: National Council of Teachers of Mathematics.

Fennell, F., B.M. Kobett, & J. A. Wray. 2017. *The Formative 5: Everyday Assessment Techniques for Every Math Classroom.* Thousand Oaks, CA: Corwin; Reston, VA: National Council of Teachers of Mathematics.

Jacobs, V.R., L.L.C. Lamb, R.A. Philipp, & B.P. Schappelle. 2011. "Deciding How to Respond on the Basis of Children's Understandings." In *Mathematics Teacher Noticing: Seeing Through Teachers' Eyes*, eds. M.G. Sherin, V.R. Jacobs, & R.A. Philipp, 97–116. New York: Routledge.

Krechevksy, M., B. Mardell, M. Rivard, & D. Wilson. 2013. *Visible Learners: Promoting Reggio-Inspired Approaches in All Schools.* San Francisco, CA: Jossey-Bass.

OGAP Math LLC. 2017. "OGAP Additive Framework." www.ogapmath.com/wp-content/uploads/2017/04/framework_November2017.pdf.

Sherin, M.G., & E.A. van Es. 2003. "A New Lens on Teaching: Learning to Notice." *Mathematics Teaching in the Middle School* 9 (2): 92–95.

Tapper, J. 2012. *Solving for Why: Understanding, Assessing, and Teaching Students Who Struggle with Math, Grades K–8.* Sausalito, CA: Math Solutions.

Wiliam, D. 2017. *Embedded Formative Assessment.* 2nd ed. Bloomington, IN: Solution Tree.

About the Authors

Sarah Roller Dyess is associate professor in the department of curriculum and instruction at the University of Alabama in Huntsville.

Elizabeth Petit Cunningham is associate professor in the education department at the University of Michigan-Flint.

Katherine Ariemma Marin is assistant professor in the department of elementary, middle, and secondary teacher education at the University of Louisville.

Photographs: p. 78, © Getty Images; pp. 79, 81, 82, courtesy of the authors

PART THREE

Assessment Practices to Support Inclusion

NAEYC's position statement on advancing equity in early childhood education asserts that "all children have the right to equitable learning opportunities that enable them to achieve their full potential as engaged learners and valued members of society" (NAEYC 2019, 1). Take a moment to think about your own classroom. How does it reflect this statement? How do you know? Documenting and assessing children's strengths, practices, development, ideas, and abilities helps to make these inclusive and equitable practices visible.

The four articles in this part offer a look at a variety of assessment practices that support inclusion in the classroom and help programs ensure they are providing equitable learning opportunities and building on all children's strengths.

In "Assessing Opportunities to Support Each Child: 12 Practices for Quality Inclusion," **Camille Catlett** and **Elena P. Soukakou** share best practices to support all learners in the classroom. These practices promote an equitable environment and positive interactions, all based on deep reviews of research as well as direct experience in classroom application.

Christan G. Coogle, Emily M. Rose, Jennifer R. Ottley, Jennifer A. Brown, and **Mollie K. Romano** describe a five-step, data-informed process for individualized and inclusive education in their article, "Embedded Learning Opportunities for Children with and Without Disabilities." This process of creating embedded learning opportunities within everyday classroom activities and routines supports meaningful instruction for all children in a classroom.

In "Authentic and Meaningful Developmental Screening in Early Childhood," **Marisa Macy** and **Stefano J. Bagnato** discuss the value of using "screening with meaning," how to implement developmental screenings, and talking with families through the process.

The final article in the collection is by **Janet L. Gooch,** titled "Enhancing Toddlers' Communication Skills: Partnerships with Speech-Language Pathologists." She writes about building partnerships with resources in the community to support classroom teachers with language development strategies for toddlers.

REFERENCE

NAEYC. 2019. "Advancing Equity in Early Childhood Education." Position statement. Washington, DC: NAEYC. www.naeyc.org/resources/position-statements/equity.

Assessing Opportunities to Support Each Child

12 Practices for Quality Inclusion

Camille Catlett and Elena P. Soukakou

The newest member of Ms. Dorina's preschool classroom is Taylor, who is 3 years old and full of life. Balls, cars, and anything that makes noise are his favorite playthings. Until recently, Taylor had received early intervention services at home. He has made terrific progress since he was first diagnosed with an autism spectrum disorder, but he still has significant delays in receptive and expressive language and in social and emotional development.

When Taylor's parents met with Ms. Dorina last week, they mentioned that because of his language delays, Taylor sometimes has difficulty interacting with adults, expressing his needs and feelings, and connecting with other children. His parents also shared that Taylor is usually interested in what other children are doing, but he finds it difficult to engage in play with his peers.

Ms. Dorina counts on Ms. Laura, Taylor's speech-language pathologist, for ideas about ways to support Taylor within classroom routines. Still, Ms. Dorina finds herself wondering, *How can I make my classroom welcoming and supportive for Taylor? How can I help Taylor to make friends and play with his classmates? And how can we all work together in ways that support Taylor and all of the other children too?*

Over the past two decades, research on early childhood inclusion has enabled a greater understanding of how we can best support the learning needs of young children with identified disabilities in early childhood classrooms. Research findings on the effectiveness of high-quality inclusion, along with innovations that are generated in everyday practice, have equipped us with rich knowledge, support systems, and resources for meeting the needs of young learners (Odom, Buysse, & Soukakou 2011). But how can we proactively assess opportunities to support the unique needs of a young learner like Taylor?

Assessing Environments, Interactions, and Supports for Quality Inclusion

The joint position statement of the Division of Early Childhood of the Council for Exceptional Children (DEC) and NAEYC on early childhood inclusion states that the desired results of inclusive experiences for children with and without disabilities are "a sense of belonging and membership, positive social relationships and friendships, and development and learning to reach their full potential" (DEC & NAEYC 2009, 2). This means that our efforts need to focus on quality experiences for *each* child (e.g., Taylor) and for *every* child (i.e., every other child in Taylor's class, as well as Taylor).

The position statement reminds us that achieving quality inclusion requires effectively using practices that support young children to access and fully participate in opportunities to learn, develop, and connect. What practices can early childhood educators use every day in their classrooms to meet the needs of each and every young learner?

In the following sections, we share a synthesis of 12 practices, drawn from extensive research, classroom application, and review, that are essential for establishing quality environments, interactions, and supports (Odom, Buysse, & Soukakou 2011; Soukakou 2016). For each practice, there is a set of specific strategies that can be used in an early childhood program.

Recently, a classroom observation tool—the Inclusive Classroom Profile (ICP)—was developed to support early childhood educators, specialists, administrators, professional development providers, and families to assess what is happening in the classroom and to use that information to enhance opportunities for each child—particularly for children with disabilities (Soukakou 2016). The ICP is a structured observation measure that assesses 12 inclusive practices that can support the developmental and learning needs of children with identified disabilities in early childhood programs. The ICP was conceptualized by the second author of this article; she is a researcher and trained early childhood special educator with experience in inclusive early childhood programs. The ICP's development was based on the best available research on effective classroom practices for supporting inclusion in early childhood, along with extensive research and collaboration with early childhood educators and program administrators. The ICP has been studied and used successfully in a wide range of early childhood programs (Soukakou et al. 2015).

Each item of the ICP represents a different area of practice and includes a set of quality indicators that guide users in assessing the quality of specific inclusive strategies. To conduct an ICP assessment, users need to observe a classroom's planned daily activities and routines for three hours in order to observe a wide range of classroom activities, routines, and interactions between adults and children. A short interview with the classroom teacher is also needed to gather additional information on some of the instructional strategies and supports that were observed on the day of the assessment. Information gathered using the ICP can help in assessing the extent to which inclusive practices were used in the classroom to meet the needs of a specific child with identified disabilities, while also paying attention to the active participation and engagement of all children in the classroom.

In this way, the ICP can be used as a tool to support early childhood professionals to assess and monitor the use of inclusive teaching strategies and guide instructional decisions and supports for each and every child. The authors of this article have been working together to support early childhood professionals to become familiar with the practices outlined in the ICP and to use those practices to effectively include all children in their classrooms.

Practices that Support Each and Every Child

What follows is an overview of each of the 12 ICP practices. With each practice come essential questions for educators to ask to inspire reflection, support decision making, and inform assessment of the practice's impact. We then return to Taylor to provide more detailed examples of how each practice might be implemented to support a specific child.

Practice 1: Adaptations of Space, Materials, and Equipment

Practice 1 involves assessing how physical space, materials, and equipment in a classroom are organized, placed, and used every day by adults and children. When adults prepare physical environments, it is important to set them up in ways that are accessible to all children. It is equally important to intentionally organize the space, materials, and equipment throughout the day to support each child's individual and social experiences. For a child who uses a walker to move around the classroom independently, it may mean monitoring how the other children use and put away toys to support their classmate's movement from one area of the room to another.

Adults can also observe the classroom and reflect on how materials and equipment are placed or adapted to support each child in independently using them. Can all children use materials and equipment independently? At the same time, adults can monitor how children use materials and can provide the necessary scaffolding to help children use the materials in meaningful ways. For a child who has difficulty with fine motor skills, such as cutting with scissors, a teacher might provide hand-over-hand assistance to help them use scissors to cut out a shape. Likewise, a teacher might need to monitor how a child attempts to use finger paint for the first time and be ready to model some options, if needed.

Practice 2: Adult Involvement in Peer Interactions

Practice 2 involves assessing opportunities to use specific strategies to help children initiate and sustain relationships with other children. Opportunities for adult involvement can range from organizing social activities, interactions, and games to intentionally encouraging children to participate in those activities, particularly children for whom interacting socially might be challenging. For children who might have difficulty initiating or maintaining social engagements with their peers, the ICP reminds us that teachers may use more specific scaffolding strategies, such as modeling and offering verbal or nonverbal prompts to a child to help them respond to a friend. For example, during free-play time, a teacher could model how to take turns throwing and catching a ball to support a child for whom taking turns in play is difficult. Another scaffolding strategy might involve enlisting other peers to help children for whom interacting socially is challenging. For example, a teacher could pair two children for a finger-painting activity and teach a child how to help their peer engage in the activity.

Practice 3: Adults' Guidance of Children's Free-Choice Activities and Play

Practice 3 involves assessing how to support children's active and sustained engagement in both individual and social play activities. This may involve considering how we monitor children's selection of activities and playmates and the ways children engage in play. It may also involve individualizing

supports for children who have difficulty engaging in activities. One child might need support to become engaged in an activity while another child might need adult help to engage in collaborative problem solving during social play activities with their peers.

Monitoring how children engage in activities, showing availability during free-play time, and using specific scaffolding strategies are some specific ICP strategies that teachers can use to support active engagement in play. For example, for a child with attention difficulties, a teacher might use a visual activity map to help the child focus more easily on each step of an art activity. For another child who is using blocks to construct an imaginary hospital, a teacher might extend the play by asking open-ended questions and helping the child form hypotheses and make connections between ideas. In both of these examples, the teacher uses strategies to meet a child's individual needs while also enabling the child to participate meaningfully in the activity of their choice. The teacher may take photographs or keep observation notes to monitor how children respond to these strategies and then adjust their planning for each child.

Practice 4: Conflict Resolution

As children engage in activities and social relationships with their peers, they also learn to negotiate their differences and resolve their conflicts. Adults play an important role in supporting children in this process. What are thoughtful ways that adults can listen to children and acknowledge their perspectives, support children to communicate their feelings, and help children find alternative, appropriate ways to interact with their peers? To effectively promote conflict resolution, each of these requires strategies. As an illustration, a teacher might help a child who is nonverbal to use sign language or a communication board to talk about a conflict that occurred. Clear rules and behavior expectations that are established and communicated consistently between adults and across routines are essential to encourage positive social behavior.

Practice 5: Membership

A key aspect of quality inclusion involves creating a classroom community in which each and every child feels welcome and has a sense of membership and belonging. This means creating an inclusive social climate in which individual differences are recognized and accepted, offering children equal opportunities to assume various roles and responsibilities in the classroom, and supporting children to make choices about themselves and the whole group. The ICP reminds us that recognizing and accepting children's individual differences requires intentionally planning activities that promote understanding and acceptance of diversity as well as using strategies in the moment to respond to children's individual differences in inclusive ways.

For example, when the class is voting on an upcoming class trip, the teacher might use visual cues to help a child with a significant social and communication disorder understand the options and express their choice. Understanding the tools that build membership will bolster each teacher's ability to support quality inclusive environments and to build opportunities for any child who is new to the setting to fully participate.

Practice 6: Relationships Between Adults and Children

One of the most consistent findings of child development research is the importance of positive, responsive, and reciprocal social interactions between adults and children. How can adults consistently observe children to learn how to be highly responsive to their interests and emotional needs and concerns? Here's one way: a teacher who notices a child expressing their fear of thunderstorms might start a conversation during which the teacher validates the child's feelings, listens to their thoughts, and shows availability to sustain the conversation. This attention to building and sustaining connections between adults and children can also support children who may be new to the classroom. Being consistently available and responsive to children's interests and concerns may be essential for a child who has experienced trauma or another challenging life circumstance.

Through sustained social interactions with children, adults can extend children's play and activities and scaffold their learning. For example, a teacher watching two children watering plants in the class's garden might join them and ask open-ended questions to build vocabulary, extend their understanding of certain ideas, and help them make connections between their actions.

Practice 7: Support for Communication

Children with communication disorders can benefit from strategies that help them express their needs, communicate with their peers, and engage in classroom routines and activities. The same can be true for children who are dual language learners building their vocabulary and grammar in the language of the classroom. What strategies might a teacher use to encourage and support children's communication? This might mean that a teacher models for a child how to make a request or offers verbal prompts to help a child respond to their peer. Or a teacher might use visuals (real objects, photos) to support children's vocabulary development and to encourage all children to participate during circle time. Daily observation of children in a classroom of diverse young learners can lead a teacher to the selection of more effective strategies.

Practice 8: Adaptations of Group Activities

Assessing ways to adapt group activities throughout the day is essential for actively engaging and effectively supporting learning needs in a group. In what ways can a teacher adapt whole and small group activities to support each child's participation? Effective practices often involve adjusting the size of the group, adapting the materials of the activity, or individualizing the learning goals and strategies. For example, during story time with a small group of children, a teacher might encourage the participation of a child with a language disorder by reading an adapted book of the same story that includes less text and supplement this with concrete props on a felt board. Later, to scaffold learning, the same teacher might repeat the beginning, middle, and end of the story, using props to support the child's understanding of the sequence of story events. Understanding the different ways a teacher can support each child's participation can help teachers differentiate their support for each child, as needed.

Practice 9: Transitions Between Activities

Transitions between activities and routines are an important learning context. In an early childhood program, common transitions might involve moving from a free-choice activity time to group story time. For a child with a disability, it might also involve rejoining classmates after participating in a small therapy group. Many young children find transitions challenging, as they are often required to stop doing something they enjoy, wait for the next activity, move to a different physical location, or interact with different adults and/or children. What specific strategies can be used to support transitions? Adults can assess the extent to which they use proactive strategies with the whole group, such as marking the beginning and end of activities with songs, switching lights off and on during transitions, or using a timer to remind children of upcoming activities. Adults can also use individualized strategies for some children who have difficulty making transitions between activities. For example, a teacher might use an individualized picture schedule with a child to help them prepare for the next activity.

Practice 10: Feedback

Constructive comments about how children think, participate, and engage in different tasks are important. What type of feedback is most likely to support each child's learning? And more important, how can feedback be provided to individual children to support their motivation to learn? The nature, frequency, and ways in which adults embed different types of feedback in their interactions with children can have a significant impact on learning and emotional development. In quality inclusive classrooms, teachers focus their feedback on children's efforts rather than on children's end products. Teachers who create inclusive classrooms also adjust the form of feedback according to each child's needs. For example, a teacher might high-five all children as a form of feedback, with a specific eye toward reinforcing a child who is deaf.

Practice 11: Family-Professional Partnerships

An essential characteristic of high-quality inclusion is a successful partnership between families and early childhood educators. What roles can families play in a program's efforts to include a child with a disability? They can be partners in planning, documenting, and reflecting on effective inclusion strategies in their homes and in everyday family routines. As they do so, they contribute important information about their child's needs and progress, as well as share ideas about supportive interventions.

Likewise, early childhood educators can support families by working closely together to reflect on documentation for the classroom, exchange perspectives, communicate on a regular basis, and support each other in meeting children's identified goals. Imagine, for example, that a family is concerned about bringing a child who is on the autism spectrum to an upcoming family reunion. A conversation between family members and staff could lead to an effective plan, especially if the teacher is able to share detailed evidence of strategies that have helped the child engage in whole group interactions in the classroom.

Practice 12: Monitoring Children's Learning

Having a system for reviewing the strategies and learning supports that are used in a child's classroom and home enables everyone involved to assess what practices have been helpful for each child and to make adjustments as needed. How do early childhood educators know if they are meeting

Resources to Support Inclusive Practices and Decisions

Here are some free, online resources that can support a formative assessment process and the use of ICP practices in inclusive settings.

CONNECT Module 1: Embedded Interventions (https://connectmodules.dec-sped.org/connect-modules/learners/module-1)

In this module, educators learn about ways to incorporate practices into daily routines to help children participate in a variety of early learning opportunities and environments. All resources are available in English, Spanish, Portuguese, and Mandarin, including downloadable video clips that illustrate evidence-based practices and components of inclusion. One of the videos, "Reading at Circle Time," is described here:

> This short video, in both English and Spanish, shows how Jacob's teacher has worked with his speech-language pathologist to incorporate specific supports for his learning and participation. As you watch, you'll see how materials have been adapted. You'll also see how this approach is supporting both Jacob and his peers. By monitoring Jacob's participation in the activity, his teacher will be able to gather data on how frequently he is producing his target sounds accurately and be able to work with his therapist to make adjustments.

Resources Supporting Individualization for Children Ages Birth to 5 (https://eclkc.ohs.acf.hhs.gov/children-disabilities/article/resources-supporting-individualization)

This collection of resources provides information about evidence-based practices that support individualized decisions for children with and without disabilities. These practices are aligned with the Head Start Early Learning Outcomes Framework (https://eclkc.ohs.acf.hhs.gov/school-readiness/article/head-start-early-learning-outcomes-framework). The resources are organized around the eight topic areas of evidence-based practices identified in the Division for Early Childhood Recommended Practices (www.dec-sped.org/dec-recommended-practices). The recommended practices have been validated as having the strongest evidence base for individualizing teaching and learning opportunities for all children.

a child's learning and developmental needs? Developing an intervention plan for each child that lists goals and specific strategies and interventions can be an effective tool for monitoring a child's progress in a more holistic manner.

Regularly gathering rich information about the context and ways in which individual children respond to adult scaffolding can be an effective way to assess how each child learns, and it can help teachers adjust their support. For example, to reflect on a nonverbal child's progress with conflict resolution, a teacher may want to create a running record that lists the different ways they have been helping the child express their perspective and feelings during instances of peer conflict. The teacher can also highlight the strategies that seemed to help the child communicate their feelings to their peers.

Supporting Taylor: Reflection Questions and Strategies for Implementing Inclusive Practices

How Can I Use the Environment to Support Each Child?	
Practice 1: Adaptations of space, materials, and equipment	Because Ms. Dorina knows how much Taylor loves balls, she decides to use balls during circle time as part of a group language game. In this activity, each child, including Taylor, is verbally encouraged to roll a ball to a peer sitting nearby and to then greet the classmate by name. By observing Taylor's engagement in this activity over time, Ms. Dorina can monitor ways to scaffold his successful participation in increasingly challenging activities.
How Can I Engage and Support Each Child in Routines and Activities?	
Practice 3: Adults' guidance of children's free-choice activities and play	During free-choice time, Taylor often enjoys playing in the block area. One morning, Ms. Dorina notices that Taylor is interested in a block structure that some of his friends are building, and she helps him create a similar structure using a visual map.
Practice 8: Adaptations of group activities	Right before the end of free-choice time, Ms. Dorina gently reminds Taylor of the upcoming activities and reviews with him the classroom's picture schedule to help him prepare for music time.
Practice 9: Transitions between activities	When Taylor starts helping to put the blocks away, Ms. Dorina comments positively on his effort to help his friends clean up. She explains to the whole group how a team effort helps clear space for them to move around in their upcoming music and dance activity.
Practice 10: Feedback	During circle time at the end of the day, Ms. Dorina asks the children to reflect on their favorite activities of the day. To encourage children to express their choices, Ms. Dorina asks each child to show the others the activity or game they enjoyed playing most.
How Can I Identify What Works (and What Doesn't Work) to Support Each Child?	
Practice 12: Monitoring children's learning	Ms. Dorina and Ms. Laura (the speech-language pathologist) have scheduled regular meetings to compare observation notes, photographs, and other documentation showing how Taylor approaches new learning tasks and situations. They'll use this information to make adjustments to their strategies and supports and will share what they learn with Taylor's family.

Using These Practices Together to Assess Opportunities

A significant body of research indicates that these specialized instructional practices provide a strong foundation for quality inclusion (NPDCI 2011; Odom, Buysse, & Soukakou 2011). By intentionally evaluating if, when, and how these practices are being used in the classroom, early childhood educators can identify opportunities to better support each child's active participation and unique learning and developmental needs. To see how the practices are woven into daily routines and interactions that support Taylor's full participation, see "Supporting Taylor: Reflection Questions and Strategies for Implementing Inclusive Practices," on pages 96–97.

How Can I Build Relationships with and Among the Children?	
Practice 2: Adult involvement in peer interactions **Practice 4:** Conflict resolution **Practice 6:** Relationships between adults and children **Practice 7:** Support for communication	To support both Taylor and his classmates, Ms. Dorina has a flexible morning greeting system. All of the children can indicate how they want to be greeted as they enter the room: with a hug, a wave, or a high five. Taylor used to select a wave every day, but he has recently been high-fiving Ms. Dorina each morning. To support Taylor in connecting with other children, Ms. Dorina asks Caleb, a classmate who enjoys playing with Taylor, to help. With Ms. Dorina's support, every morning after circle time Caleb helps Taylor choose which activity area he wants to play in by using a set of picture symbols. Ms. Dorina stays nearby and observes as Taylor makes his choice. During free-choice time, Ms. Dorina encourages Taylor to join some activities with his peers. One morning, Ms. Dorina observes Taylor engaged in a conflict with another child over some blocks they both want to use. Ms. Dorina gently approaches the children, acknowledges their frustration, and invites them to share their feelings. She then offers two options from their collaboratively developed "Classroom Solutions" folder for how to share the blocks. Later, at snack time, Ms. Dorina joins Taylor and his classmate in a conversation about their earlier play with blocks. She then encourages the other children to join in to share and discuss things that happened earlier in the day.
How Can I Build a Community that Engages, Reflects, and Supports Each Unique Child and Family?	
Practice 5: Membership **Practice 11:** Family-professional partnerships	Morning meeting in Ms. Dorina's class includes opportunities to welcome each child and to prepare for a successful day. As part of a greeting song, children may say hello using English, sign language, picture symbols, or Tagalog (spoken by one of Taylor's classmates) to honor differences and to build membership. Ms. Dorina and Ms. Laura use a digital camera to document classroom activities. Most days they send photos via email to each family with information about the activities. They find this to be an effective way to support carryover and cohesion between home and program. By checking in with Taylor's family, Ms. Dorina and Ms. Laura get information about what Taylor is sharing, how often, and with whom. This additional information about Taylor's progress will help his teachers make decisions about what they do in the classroom.

Reflection Questions

1. The inclusive practices Ms. Dorina used with Taylor are illustrated in "Supporting Taylor: Reflection Questions and Strategies for Implementing Inclusive Practices" on pages 96–97. Think about each of the questions and the associated practices outlined there for the children you teach:
   - How can I use the environment to support each child?
   - How can I engage and support each child in routines and activities?
   - How can I identify what works (and what doesn't work) to support each child?
   - How can I build relationships with and among the children?
   - How can I build a community that engages, reflects, and supports each unique child and family?
2. In answering the previous questions, what did you learn about yourself as an early childhood educator? What did you learn about your process of understanding and supporting each and every child in your classroom?
3. How can you use the quality indicators on the ICP to build a more inclusive curriculum?

Conclusion

The practices described in this article are drawn from the Inclusive Classroom Profile, a classroom observation tool designed to assess the quality of inclusive classroom practices in early childhood settings (Soukakou 2016). The article offers evidence-based insights—based on the ICP—to help educators observe, select, adjust, individualize, and revise practices to support each and every child. The resources offered in "Resources to Support Inclusive Practices and Decisions" on page 95 share additional examples of how to use evidence-based practices to support all children.

REFERENCES

DEC (Division for Early Childhood of the Council for Exceptional Children) & NAEYC. 2009. "Early Childhood Inclusion." Joint position statement. Chapel Hill: The University of North Carolina, FPG Child Development Institute. https://npdci.fpg.unc.edu/sites/npdci.fpg.unc.edu/files/resources/EarlyChildhoodInclusion_0.pdf.

NPDCI (National Professional Development Center on Inclusion). 2011. *Research Synthesis Points on Quality Inclusive Practices*. Chapel Hill, NC: UNC, FPG Child Development Institute. https://npdci.fpg.unc.edu/sites/npdci.fpg.unc.edu/files/resources/NPDCI-ResearchSynthesisPointsInclusivePractices-2011_0.pdf.

Odom, S.L., V. Buysse, & E. Soukakou. 2011. "Inclusion for Young Children with Disabilities: A Quarter Century of Research Perspectives." *Journal of Early Intervention* 33 (4): 344–56.

Soukakou, E.P. 2016. *The Inclusive Classroom Profile (ICP) Manual, Research Edition*. Baltimore: Brookes.

Soukakou, E.P., P.J. Winton, T.A. West, J.H. Sideris, & L.M. Rucker. 2015. "Measuring the Quality of Inclusive Practices: Findings from the Inclusive Classroom Profile Pilot." *Journal of Early Intervention* 36 (3): 223–40.

About the Authors

Camille Catlett, MA, is a consultant based at the Frank Porter Graham Child Development Institute, where she works with colleges and universities to improve how early childhood professionals are prepared to work with children and families of diverse cultures, languages, and abilities.

Elena P. Soukakou, PhD, is an honorary research fellow of the School of Education, University of Roehampton, in the United Kingdom. Elena works closely with universities, professional development organizations, and early childhood professionals to support aspects of quality inclusion in early childhood programs.

Embedded Learning Opportunities for Children with and Without Disabilities

Christan G. Coogle, Emily M. Rose, Jennifer R. Ottley, Jennifer A. Brown, and Mollie K. Romano

Three-year-old Emma attends an inclusive preschool classroom alongside 13 other children—three with disabilities and 10 without. Emma was recently diagnosed with autism spectrum disorder, and while she has many strengths, she is not yet communicating with words. Emma's teacher, Marcy, has been working with Emma toward a target skill of using words. Today, Marcy has purposefully placed some blocks on the rug in the block center in front of her where Emma can see them but cannot reach them. Marcy's goal is that this "in-sight-but-out-of-reach" strategy may cause Emma to use words to communicate that she wants the blocks.

When Emma begins her play, Marcy soon notices she wants the blocks that are out of reach as Emma begins looking toward the blocks and reaching for them. Marcy intentionally waits, giving Emma time to try using words to express her desire for the blocks. Knowing that Emma has not accomplished the target skill before, Marcy is prepared to offer support if or when necessary. After waiting three seconds, Marcy provides a verbal prompt for Emma to use words by modeling, "Blocks." Marcy waits three more seconds to see if Emma will imitate. When Emma does not imitate her, Marcy again models saying, "Blocks," and then provides the desired blocks. Marcy knows the most important thing is to sustain the interaction with Emma, which is why she provides Emma with the desired item (blocks) after modeling. Over time, Emma will begin to imitate and eventually use the word "blocks" spontaneously.

Individualization is a key component of high-quality, inclusive early education. To plan and use practices that implement individualized teaching and learning, educators like Marcy offer children with and without disabilities multiple and varied opportunities to learn and grow during their daily activities and routines (Johnson, Rahn, & Bricker 2015). This aligns with NAEYC's recent position statement on developmentally appropriate practice, which states that educators "are prepared to individualize their teaching strategies to meet the specific needs of individual children, including children with disabilities and children whose learning is advanced, by building upon their interests, knowledge, and skills" (2020, 12).

To be effective, individualized teaching includes a child's entire educational team—teachers, specialists, and other professionals who collect assessment information, identify learning outcomes, use instructional strategies, and monitor progress. When team members work together, it is consistent, and both adults and children benefit (Spence et al. 2021).

Embedded learning opportunities are one instructional method that a team in early childhood settings can use to meet all children's needs. Embedded learning opportunities align with research-supported practices (DEC 2014; NAEYC 2020) and occur in three parts. First, an adult provides an antecedent, such as prompts or other cues, to elicit a targeted behavior or skill in a child, which may be identified ahead of time if the child has an Individualized Education Program (IEP). Second, the target behavior occurs either spontaneously (the child initiates it) or with support (the skill is prompted and/or modeled by an adult). The embedded learning opportunity concludes with the delivery of a motivating consequence, such as Marcy giving Emma the blocks in the opening vignette. Teachers who use this method offer many opportunities for children to practice target skills, helping them learn how to use those skills across multiple routines (Johnson et al. 2015).

According to the Division for Early Childhood of the Council for Exceptional Children (DEC; 2014), effective embedded learning opportunities are

- Based on a child's participation in everyday activities and routines
- Target specific skills
- Embedded throughout daily activities and routines
- Delivered as planned

In this article, we describe a five-step, data-informed process to help teachers find ways to create embedded learning opportunities within everyday classroom activities and routines and to ensure all children's inclusion in the classroom community (NAEYC 2020). This process also provides adaptations that can be used by teachers like Marcy who have children with varying abilities—including children with and without disabilities—in their early childhood settings such as elementary classrooms, family child care, and center-based programs.

Step One: Gathering Meaningful Data Through Authentic Assessment

Marcy arranged to meet with Emma's family as soon as Emma enrolled in the preschool program, and she continues to meet with them during the year. At one meeting, Marcy asks, "What are your hopes and dreams for Emma?" Emma's mother shares that she would love to be able to better understand Emma. She indicates that communication is a challenge because Emma is using sounds that her family does not understand. Her father nods in agreement. Marcy follows up by saying, "I hear you saying that you would really like to be able to more effectively communicate with Emma. Am I hearing you correctly?" Emma's mother and father say yes.

Based on the information the family provides, Marcy decides to use observations to determine how Emma is currently communicating within classroom activities and routines. Collecting this type of information will help Marcy to understand Emma's communication in her daily environment so Marcy can create suitable learning opportunities.

The next day, Marcy sets out to observe Emma's communication. During the class's daily snack time, Emma eats yogurt. Today, Marcy gives Emma a spoon and bowl, but she "forgets" the expected yogurt to see if and how Emma will ask for it. Marcy records her observations and has a journal ready to document Emma's engagement.

The first step when creating embedded learning opportunities is to collect information about the child so teachers can make intentional, developmentally, and contextually appropriate decisions when working toward a target skill (DEC 2014; NAEYC 2020). This includes gathering information during everyday activities and routines about the child's behavior, knowledge, interests, preferences, and social and cultural contexts. Teachers can do this through observation and by using checklists, rating scales, family interviews, work samples, and other techniques to learn about the children in their classrooms and the families they serve.

Observations can be particularly helpful and can occur live or via audio or video recordings to help teachers learn about a child's participation and engagement in various routines and activities. Observations can occur during lunchtime, outdoor time, and instructional times. Teachers may arrange circumstances so they can observe a child's behavior or skill in a situation that would not usually occur on its own (Bagnato, Neisworth, & Pretti-Frontczak 2010)—such as Marcy forgetting to give Emma yogurt. Having an informal checklist or anecdotal record ready can assist teachers in quickly documenting these types of observations.

Family interviews are another helpful way to gather important information about a child and to better understand a child's social and cultural contexts. Teachers can ask families about their child, their family dynamics, and any questions, hopes, or priorities they have regarding their child. Family interviews can occur when a child first joins an early education program and can continue throughout the year.

Step Two: Using Data to Identify Learning Goals and Outcomes for Embedded Instruction

After observing and recording data, teachers use the information they have gathered to develop learning goals. These goals should "recognize individual variation in learners and allow children to demonstrate their competencies in different ways" (NAEYC 2020, 20). They should also align with a program's overarching curriculum and a child's context, strengths, and interests. Once teachers know what goal they are working toward, they can embed learning opportunities throughout the day to help children reach the goals. Learning goals must be clearly defined and recorded in planning documents, such as in a child's IEP if applicable.

Embedded learning opportunities should include three components (Johnson et al. 2015):

- **Behavior:** This should be observable and measurable, meaning that it can be seen or heard and documented. For instance, it would be difficult to collect data on the outcome *Emma will demonstrate conversational skills* because an observable behavior is not included. (What does she do to demonstrate conversational skills?) A measurable alternative is *Emma will use single words*, which can be observed and documented.

  Besides being measurable, the targeted, observable behavior should also support a child becoming adaptive, socially connected, and engaged in their learning environment (DEC 2014). For example, *Emma will use words so that she can communicate wants and needs* is related to engagement; *Emma will use 10 different words* is not. Adding the functional statement *so that Emma can communicate wants and needs* helps ensure that the learning goal engages Emma in her everyday environment.

- **Condition:** Teachers should specify the context in and circumstances under which the measurable behavior will occur. Will it be during lunch, free play, or other routine activities, or will the skill occur when prompted by the teacher? For example, *Emma will use words when provided opportunities to communicate a choice.*

- **Criterion:** How will teachers measure success? For example, *Emma will use words to express her wants or needs a minimum of three times per day*. When Emma is able to meet this criterion of using words to communicate three times a day, then she will have successfully achieved the learning goal.

Marcy's observations have given her a rich picture of Emma. Marcy sees that Emma enjoys playing in the block center. She builds detailed structures and incorporates a variety of toys such as cars, people, and dinosaurs. She engages with materials for a sustained period of time, uses gestures such as pointing and reaching, and vocalizes sounds to comment and request.

Her observations also indicate that Emma's difficulty communicating her wants and needs using words is causing frustration. Marcy turns to the rest of Emma's educational team so they can outline Emma's learning goals together. Her team consists of her mother, father, teacher, and speech language pathologist who will work together to support Emma to reach her learning goal. The team determines the following goal to be appropriate for Emma: *When provided opportunities to make a choice, Emma will use single words to communicate wants and needs a minimum of three times per day.* This goal includes a condition statement (*when provided opportunities to make a choice*), a measurable behavior that will help Emma become adaptive, socially connected, and engaged in her environment (*will use single words to communicate wants and needs*), and a criterion (*three times per day*).

Creating Embedded Learning Opportunities for Emma

5-Step Process	A Step-by-Step Plan
Step 1 Gathering data	Emma's preschool teacher, Marcy, collaborates with Emma's parents to support her social and communication development. Marcy meets with Emma's mother during a home visit and asks about Emma's social interaction and communication with her family at home. Emma's mother shares that Emma rarely engages in activities. She also shares that Emma enjoys stories.
Step 2 Using data to identify learning outcomes	Marcy and Emma's mother want to focus on helping Emma be able to make a choice throughout daily activities and routines. To do this, Emma will begin by using gestures like pointing and single words to make a choice and to comment.
Step 3 Planning and using embedded learning opportunities	Marcy will create opportunities for Emma to communicate throughout daily activities and routines. Marcy will offer Emma choices between books or instruments, use wait time, and model language targets (antecedents). When Emma approximates single words (behavior), Marcy will expand and extend her language and provide her with the desired activity, material, or action (consequence).
Step 4 Implementation fidelity	Marcy will gather data on the embedded opportunities she is creating for Emma during daily activities and routines.
Step 5 Monitoring progress	Marcy will monitor Emma's progress through documentation of Emma's use of single word approximations and words throughout daily activities and routines. Marcy will share the graphed data with Emma's mother to discuss patterns and progress toward Emma's goal.

Step Three: Planning and Using Embedded Learning Opportunities

Armed with Emma's learning goals, the team looks at Marcy's daily classroom plans and scripts out strategies to propel Emma toward meeting those goals, including ways she can adjust Emma's environment and questions that she can ask Emma. The team identifies different activities throughout the day when they can offer choices and determines who will offer them. The activities they decide on include circle time, child-led play, and mealtime.

During circle time, Marcy can provide a choice between two types of materials or activities (musical instruments, books). The individuals to facilitate embedded learning opportunities can include teachers, family members, and classmates.

During child-led play, another child can offer a choice between areas of the room or centers in which Emma would like to engage (blocks, dramatic play).

During mealtime, Marcy or Emma's parent can give choices so Emma can select what she would like to drink (milk, juice).

Once the team develops measurable learning goals, they can plan for, design, and begin to implement an embedded learning opportunity (Johnson et al. 2015) within everyday activities and routines that is aligned with a child's IEP goals, if applicable.

To do this, the team must review their plan of when to provide the opportunity and who is responsible for it. It is also beneficial to review the plan regularly to determine how it is working and any changes that need to be made. To be effective, team members must regularly use embedded learning opportunities and increase the number of times the child has to practice and attain targeted skills. If the child has a team of providers (special education teacher, speech-language pathologist), the teacher must ensure they are familiar with the embedded learning opportunity and understand how to use it (Snyder et al. 2015). Specific tools, such as an activity matrix, can help ensure this occurs (Sandall & Schwartz 2008). (See "Activity Matrix for Emma" on page 106 for an example.)

Throughout the embedded learning opportunity process, teachers are continually planning and evaluating the appropriateness of a child's learning goals, the authenticity or meaningfulness of the learning opportunity's prompts and other cues, and the effectiveness of the feedback, follow-up support, and consequences offered. Completing the full cycle of an embedded learning opportunity (antecedent; target behavior; consequence) is essential, and multiple learning opportunities should be planned for and implemented within and across daily activities so that a child has the time and support to make progress in and outside of the early childhood setting (Johnson et al. 2015).

Activity Matrix for Emma

Target behavior: *Emma will use single words to communicate wants and needs.*

Routines	Initiator	Prompt	Behavior	Consequence
Mealtime	Teacher and family	Provide insufficient quantities of desired items	Single-word phrase ("Crackers")	Receive desired item
Outside play	Teacher and family	Provide choices ("Do you want the blue ball or red ball?," "Do you want to swing on the swing set or dig in the sandbox?")	Single-word phrase ("Blue"; "Sandbox")	Receive desired item or activity
Caregiving routines (bath time)	Family	Use wait time/time delay to turn on water (Place hand on faucet with an expectant look)	Single-word phrase ("Water")	Receive desired activity or material
Transition routines	Teacher and family	Use "mand-model" (Before opening the door, the teacher or parent waits for the child to say, "Open" and waits for a response. If a response is not provided, the teacher or parent says, "Open" and opens the door.) (Miguel 2017)	Single-word phrase ("Open")	Receive desired action

Step Four: Accurate and Consistent Implementation

Marcy wants to learn more about embedded learning opportunities, so she attends an online webinar and reviews the recording of the webinar regarding embedded learning opportunities on the Division for Early Childhood website. During this webinar, many resources are shared that she thinks will support her practice. She uses the "Embedded Instructional Practices Checklist" as a self-checklist to reflect on her practices. She also asks a peer teacher to observe and record her interactions with Emma across three routines to ensure she is using the embedded learning opportunity the way she planned. Although Marcy was initially nervous asking someone to observe her, she feels much more confident in her practice afterward. The information she and her peer collect also suggests that Marcy is delivering the embedded learning opportunities as intended.

It is important that embedded learning opportunities are delivered as planned and that teachers have supports, such as coaching and performance-based feedback, to ensure that the plan is followed consistently and accurately; that is, with *implementation fidelity*. Support can come in a variety of forms, including training paired with peer observation and feedback (Barton & Fettig 2013). If the teacher or other individuals working with the child did not implement the embedded learning opportunities as planned, they should make additional efforts to improve how the work is done, then reassess fidelity. This cycle would continue until satisfactory levels of fidelity are reached.

For example, as Marcy did, team members could create a checklist that aligns with the plan they created. They could use this checklist by asking a peer to monitor the implementation of embedded learning opportunities to determine if they are being used as intended. Both affirmative and suggestive feedback from peers is one way to support practice. Affirmative feedback should identify how and when an observer noticed an embedded learning opportunity being delivered as planned, and suggestive feedback should identify how and when an observer noticed that an embedded learning opportunity could have been delivered as planned.

Once the teacher and other individuals working with the child deliver embedded learning opportunities as planned, they can evaluate whether the instruction is benefiting the child, which is described in more detail next. To measure implementation fidelity, the team may choose to use already existing tools, such as the "Embedded Instructional Practices Checklist" (Early Childhood Technical Assistance Center 2015) or webinars offered by groups such as the Division for Early Childhood (www.dec-sped.org/learning-decks).

Step Five: Monitoring Progress Toward Targeted Learning Goals

> Marcy initially created observational notes to record implementation and Emma's progress, but she realizes she will not have the time to take notes at the level of detail she needs to make informed decisions. Instead, she creates checklists that she can use to quickly identify information that would accurately inform her decisions. The checklist outlines the routines and embedded learning opportunities that will be implemented for Emma. It also has a space to document how Emma responds as it relates to the goal.

Much thought and energy go into creating and implementing embedded learning opportunities, which lead to the question, have those efforts helped? To determine whether a child has made meaningful progress toward a set goal, educators often use formative assessments, which are intended to occur on an ongoing basis and focus on targeted behaviors or knowledge. (To learn more about formative assessments, read "What's Next? How Learning Progressions Help Teachers Support Children's Development and Learning," by Peter L. Mangione, Tamara Osborne, and Heidi Mendenhall in the July 2019 issue of *Young Children*.) Teachers and others collect and evaluate assessment information related to both the child's performance before and once the plan is implemented.

Teachers should consider two factors when monitoring progress: First, is the measurement tool quick and easy to implement within daily activities and routines? Second, is the tool sensitive to small amounts of change? The aim of progress monitoring is for data to be collected regularly. By selecting a simple tool that takes minimal time to use, such as a teacher-developed checklist like Marcy's, collecting the data will be more feasible. Additionally, by using a tool that measures outcomes in small increments, it can detect changes in performance that may represent meaningful growth. (See "Sample Progress Monitoring Tool" on page 108 for an example of a checklist.)

Often, educators find it useful to look at data visually through a graph or table; patterns can become more easily discernible that way (Lane & Gast 2014). For example, if the data (visually or otherwise) show little progress or a decline related to a targeted goal, then the team can identify a different approach. Any changes in the plan should continue to be monitored for consistency and accuracy and for any changes in the child's growth. On the other hand, if the data indicate an increase or improvement toward a targeted goal, the teacher would continue with the current plan and with progress monitoring until the goal is fully met.

Sample Progress Monitoring Tool

Goal: *When provided opportunities to make a choice, Emma will use single words to communicate wants and needs a minimum of three times per day.*

Routines	Embedded learning opportunity	Child response to opportunity	Notes
Circle time	Choice between materials	Y N P	
Child-led play	Choice between centers	Y N P	
Meals	Choice between drinks	Y N P	
Total yes: Total no: Total partial:			

Note: Y=yes (demonstrates goal); N=no (does not demonstrate goal); P=partial (partially demonstrates goal)

Reflection Questions

1. What methods and strategies do you use to gather meaningful data about the knowledge, needs, and behaviors of the children you teach? How do you prepare for gathering the data? How do you record it?
2. How do you use the data collected through observations and assessment to support the individual child? What activities could be embedded in your curriculum to provide individualized learning opportunities?
3. How do you work and collaborate with other professionals to consistently implement embedded learning opportunities?
4. In what ways do you monitor the child's progress toward learning goals?

Conclusion

Embedded learning opportunities are one way teachers can support children both with and without disabilities in their classroom. This method provides children with meaningful instruction that enhances participation as well as skill development over time and in a variety of settings. Teachers and other individuals can use the five-step process described in this article to ensure they are planning and delivering embedded learning opportunities in an instructionally and functionally sound manner with the ultimate goal of supporting children to maintain and generalize target skills.

REFERENCES

Bagnato, S.J., J.T. Neisworth, & K. Pretti-Frontczak. 2010. *LINKing Authentic Assessment and Early Childhood Intervention*. 2nd ed. Baltimore: Brookes.

Barton, E.E., & A. Fettig. 2013. "Parent-Implemented Interventions for Young Children with Disabilities: A Review of Fidelity Features." *Journal of Early Intervention* 35 (2): 194–219.

DEC (Division for Early Childhood of the Council for Exceptional Children). 2014. "DEC Recommended Practices." Los Angeles: DEC. www.dec-sped.org/dec-recommended-practices.

Early Childhood Technical Assistance Center. 2015. "Embedded Instructional Practices Checklist." http://ectacenter.org/~pdfs/decrp/INS-2_Embedded_Instruction_2017.pdf.

Gatmaitan, M., & T. Brown. 2015. "Quality in Individualized Family Service Plans: Guidelines for Practitioners, Programs, and Families." *Young Exceptional Children* 19 (2): 14–32.

Johnson, J., N.L. Rahn, & D.D. Bricker. 2015. *An Activity-Based Approach to Early Intervention*. Baltimore: Brookes.

Lane, J.D., & D. Gast. 2014. "Visual Analysis in Single Case Experimental Design Studies: Brief Review and Guidelines." *Neuropsychological Rehabilitation* 24 (3–4): 445–63.

Miguel, C.F. 2017. "The Generalization of Mands." *Analysis Verbal Behavior* 33: 191–204.

NAEYC. 2020. "Developmentally Appropriate Practice." Position statement. Washington, DC: NAEYC. www.naeyc.org/resources/position-statements/dap.

Ruble, L.A., J. McGrew, N. Dalrymple, & L.A. Jung. 2010. "Examining the Quality of IEPs for Young Children with Autism." *Journal of Autism and Developmental Disorders* 40: 1459–70.

Sandall, S.R., & I.S. Schwartz. 2008. *Building Blocks for Teaching Preschoolers with Special Needs*. 2nd ed. Baltimore: Brookes.

Snyder, P.A., S. Rakap, M.L. Hemmeter, T.W. McLaughlin, S. Sandall, & M.E. McLean. 2015. "Naturalistic Instructional Approaches in Early Learning." *Journal of Early Intervention* 37 (1): 69–97.

Spence, C.M., D. Miller, C. Corr, R.M. Santos, & B. Bentley. 2021. "When in Doubt, Reach Out: Teaming Strategies for Inclusive Early Childhood Settings." *Young Children* 76 (1): 39–49.

About the Authors

Christan G. Coogle, PhD, is associate professor of special education and early childhood special education at George Mason University in Fairfax, Virginia. Her research focuses on supporting educators' use of embedded interventions.

Emily M. Rose, PhD, CCC-SLP, is clinical assistant professor in the Department of Rehabilitation Sciences at Appalachian State University in Boone, North Carolina. She coordinates an inclusive preschool program and teaches courses in the areas of autism and preschool language disorders.

Jennifer R. Ottley, PhD, is research director for the University of Cincinnati Systems Development and Improvement Center. Jennifer supports educators to improve their instruction and intervention so that it meets the needs of each and every learner.

Jennifer A. Brown, PhD, CCC-SLP, is associate professor in the Department of Communication Sciences and Special Education at the University of Georgia in Athens, Georgia. Her research focuses on improving child communication outcomes in natural and inclusive environments through collaborative practices.

Mollie K. Romano, PhD, CCC-SLP, is associate professor in the Department of Communication Disorders and the director of the Communication and Early Childhood Research and Practice Center at Florida State University in Tallahassee, Florida. Her work focuses on professional development to support caregiver coaching approaches across Part C settings, including early care and education.

Authentic and Meaningful Developmental Screening in Early Childhood

Marisa Macy and Stefano J. Bagnato

Magnolia is attending an open house at Big Smiles Academy, where she is interested in enrolling her son, Mario, in the preschool program. Mario is a playful 35-month-old who loves animals, books, and listening to music. During the open house, Magnolia meets Ms. Angela, a lead teacher, and shares that she is concerned that Mario is not yet grasping small objects like blocks, books, and finger foods during play and routines like mealtimes. Magnolia completes an enrollment packet, and Ms. Angela arranges a time for Magnolia to bring Mario to the center for a developmental screening.

When we engage in screening and assessment practices, we observe the child or group of children, and then make sense of what we see using our understanding of child development, each child's individuality, and the contexts in which they are growing and learning.

This article addresses screening with meaning. Assessment is authentic when it is meaningful to all involved. It reflects real life, or authentic opportunities to observe children engaged in their familiar settings, with familiar people, and with familiar objects and materials. Marisa (first author) became interested in this topic as a parent when her daughter experienced screening assessment as a toddler. Stefano (second author) has studied assessments for several years as a researcher at the University of Pittsburgh. In this article, we discuss fundamental details about authentic developmental screening—what it is and the purposes it serves, who is typically engaged in the screening process, and how it is effectively used in practice. Then, we revisit the opening vignette to show meaningful developmental screening in action.

What Is a Developmental Screening, and Why Is It Used?

Screenings are a formal way of helping us understand how children are developing. They do so by comparing an individual child's current skills and behaviors to a set of established norms, or a much larger set of same-age peers. Typically, screenings are brief in length and follow specific procedures for each use. Some common tools for a developmental screening in early childhood settings are the Ages & Stages Questionnaires (ASQ), BRIGANCE, and DENVER II, to name just a few.

Developmental screenings are used for at least two reasons and as part of a larger assessment approach. Two purposes are

- To assess all children in an early childhood program to identify any concerns or difficulties they might be having with their development and/or early learning. NAEYC's Early Learning Program Standards, for example, state that "all children enrolled in the program should receive developmental screening within three months of program entry" and that screening should gauge development across domains, from health and physical to cognitive, social, and emotional development.
- To assess an individual child when a familiar caregiver like a parent has a concern about the child's development or learning. For example, a parent notices differences in their youngest child's development compared to their older children. They follow up on this concern by seeking a developmental screening from an early intervention provider in their area.

Whether prompted by a program or a family, authentic developmental screenings can help determine if a more comprehensive evaluation is warranted. Screening should not be used for diagnosis or to determine eligibility for specialized services or therapies. Because developmental screenings do not offer in-depth details about a child's knowledge, skills, or behaviors, teachers rely on other forms of assessment to plan for instruction.

Who Is Involved in a Developmental Screening?

Because of its core purposes, many different professionals are engaged in observing, documenting, and understanding young children through a developmental screening. There are at least four different sectors engaged in developmental screening:

- **General education,** which includes what occurs in many early learning programs
- **Special education,** which entails early intervention for infants and toddlers and early childhood special education for preschoolers
- **Health care,** which includes care provided by pediatricians, nurses, and other health-care professionals, such as occupational therapists
- **Social work,** which includes the services provided by social workers, behavior interventionists, and counselors

For example, developmental screenings play an important role at well-visits with pediatricians. These may be the first time a family completes a screening, providing information about their child's physical or language growth or their child's emotional responses to different situations.

Families are key participants in the screening process too. They have a unique and ongoing view of their child's learning and development. They are often the first to notice if unexpected changes occur or if something does not seem right with their child's development. Family and professional collaboration is essential when children are screened.

How Is a Developmental Screening Carried Out?

Professionals screen children to document their overall growth in a variety of areas. Family-completed measures, like the ASQ, allow a familiar home caregiver to share what they have observed and experienced with the child and share that information through a checklist, rating form, or other tool. Families may not know where to turn if they have a question or concern about their child's development. To address this, early childhood educators can conduct or help arrange for individualized developmental screenings.

Because a screening is an initial step, it is only a snapshot with a limited view. Depending on the results of the screening, a more comprehensive evaluation may be needed, where a bigger picture will be taken. For example, a child could be screened with the ASQ, which has 30 items. A more comprehensive evaluation could then be done using an instrument that has many more items with a diagnostic purpose and goes deeper than a screener can. Results of the screening compare the child in general to their same-age peers. When the results indicate a child falls outside of the expected range for their age, no final decisions or diagnoses should be made. Instead, such results require a referral to a professional for a more comprehensive and detailed assessment of all developmental domains (problem solving, communication, motor skills, and more).

Selected Developmental Screening Tools

Developmental screening tool	Age group	Areas assessed
Ages & Stages Questionnaires, Third Edition (ASQ-3)	1 to 66 months	Communication, gross motor, fine motor, problem solving, and personal-social areas
Battelle Developmental Inventory, Third Edition (BDI-3)	Birth to 8 years	Adaptive, personal-social, communication, motor, and cognitive domains
BRIGANCE Early Childhood Screen III	3 to 5 years	Academic skills/cognitive development, language development, physical development, and self-help and social and emotional skills
Developmental Indicators for the Assessment of Learning, Fourth Edition (DIAL-4)	2 years, 6 months to 5 years, 11 months	Concepts, language, and motor areas; self-help and social development
Preschool and Kindergarten Behavior Scales-Second Edition (PKBS-2)	3 to 6 years	Internalizing and externalizing behaviors, social cooperation, social interaction, and social independence

Note: The above list is a brief selection of screening tools, and many more are available. Information in the table is based on publisher websites.

Preschool educators have an opportunity to partner with families and other professionals in the screening process. Sometimes educators begin the conversation with families. For example, an early learning program may use the ASQ at the start of each program year, then again toward the middle and/or end of the school year. Before a formal screening, educators can begin by sharing with families what screening is and what they can expect.

Sometimes educators start the conversation about screening because a family expresses questions or concerns. When this happens, a teacher can begin by seeking more information, asking questions like

- How would you describe your child, including their growth and learning, to someone who is unfamiliar with your child or family?
- What concerns do you have, and what do you hope to find out from the screening?
- How does your child play?
- How does your child participate in routines (washing hands, feeding, toileting, etc.)?
- How does your child interact with others?

Early childhood educators can offer support and resources for learning more about the screening goals and process. They can sit beside and get to know families. (Indeed, the origin of the word assessment comes from the Latin *assidere*, which means "to sit with.") Meaningful conversations with families are the foundation for their child's developmental screening, so it is beneficial to learn more about them in a conversational format before conducting a formal screening.

After these initial conversations and screening, the preschool educator can continue to support the family and the process. A family might need more help navigating the process if a referral was made to another agency for more in-depth diagnostic testing. Checking in with the family can be helpful.

Another next step is to assess children's development on an ongoing basis. This can include giving the screening again at specific intervals (every few months, every six months). Screening more than once over time is a useful way to monitor children's development and any concerns when they arise.

On the day of Mario's screening assessment, Magnolia makes sure he is well rested and fed. Magnolia and Mario arrive at the center, accompanied by Magnolia's best friend. Magnolia brings a list of concerns she has written about Mario's development, and an interpreter is present for the screening since English is not Magnolia's home language.

Mario appears to be comfortable and engages in tasks the way he usually does. Magnolia shares information with Ms. Angela, the preschool educator. She also asks questions and explains her concerns about Mario not yet grasping small objects like blocks, books, and finger foods. After the screening, Ms. Angela explains what will happen next in the process, including scoring and interpreting screening results and follow-up procedures.

Six days later, Ms. Angela calls Magnolia. Magnolia's intuition was right. Mario performed differently from his same-age peers in the fine motor area and how he uses his small muscles and hand-eye coordination. Later, a team of fine motor professionals, like occupational therapists, complete a comprehensive evaluation of Mario's skills. He qualifies for therapeutic services. Mario's preschool educator collaborates with specialists to embed opportunities in the classroom for him to practice fine motor skills. Ms. Angela creates activities that involve ways for Mario to strengthen the use of his hands to perform tasks with his fingers and hands. Eventually, Mario begins growing stronger in all areas of his development, especially motor. After a year, he exits specialized services. Mario enters kindergarten without a need for special education services. The meaningful screening assessment was instrumental in addressing Magnolia's concerns and in leading to appropriate further evaluation and the right support for Mario's development.

Further Resources

- Learn about the Help Me Grow model for connecting families and providers to community resources related to child development at **www.helpmegrownational.org**.
- For information on developmental milestones, see "Learn the Signs. Act Early" from the CDC, **www.cdc.gov/ncbddd/actearly/index.html**.
- Discover more about developmental screening on the podcast episode "Developmental Screenings for Young Children: What Parents and Teachers Need to Know" from the Illinois Early Learning Project, **www.illinoisearlylearning.org/podcasts/devscreen-yc**.
- For tips on connecting families with community-based services, see *Developmental Screening in Your Community: An Integrated Approach for Connecting Children with Services,* by Diane Bricker, Marisa Macy, Jane Squires, and Kevin Marks. 2013.

About the Authors

Marisa Macy, PhD, is the Cille and Ron Williams Endowed Community Chair of Early Childhood Education, Buffett Early Childhood Institute Chair, and associate professor in the Department of Teacher Education in the College of Education at the University of Nebraska Kearney.

Stefano J. Bagnato, EdD, NCSP, is a developmental school psychologist and professor of psychology and pediatrics at the University of Pittsburgh, Schools of Education and Medicine.

Reflection Questions

1. How do you "screen with meaning" in your classroom or early learning program? What familiar settings, people, and objects and materials can you incorporate in developmental screenings to make them more authentic?
2. How do you work with families to gather additional information about their children? What types of questions do you ask? What do you do with the information?
3. Think about the team of professionals (e.g., interventionists, pediatricians, social workers) you collaborate with in conducting developmental screenings. Do all of the team members have opportunities to assess the child on an ongoing basis? If not, what issues might this present?

Enhancing Toddlers' Communication Skills

Partnerships with Speech-Language Pathologists

Janet L. Gooch

Four toddlers are looking at live chicks in a box. Three of the children converse as the fourth child looks on. The teacher, Mrs. Taylor, observes the following interaction:

Olivia: What in there?

Andrew: Chicks.

Olivia: Baby chicks.

Andrew: Where's the mama chick?

Olivia: I dunno.

Ethan: Mama.

Andrew: Where's the daddy chick?

Olivia: I dunno.

Andrew: They all alone.

Olivia, Andrew, and Ethan show varying degrees of language development. Mrs. Taylor can see that the chicks are an excellent source of conversation for the children but wonders why Ricky, the fourth child, doesn't say anything. Ricky is 28 months old—the second oldest in this group. Ethan is the youngest at 22 months, while Olivia is 26 months and Andrew is 34 months.

Mrs. Taylor has questions about Ricky's language development. She has noticed that Ricky rarely talks during group activities and rarely sings during song time. Even though Ricky's mother reports that Ricky "talks all the time at home," Mrs. Taylor wonders whether Ricky needs more support. She's worried and doesn't know where to find help.

Contrast Mrs. Taylor's situation with that of Mr. Torres, a teacher in another early childhood program.

Mr. Torres is playing with Sally, a 30-month-old, when the following exchange occurs:

Mr. Torres: Where do cows live?

Sally: On a pom.

Mr. Torres: Where?

Sally: On a pom.

Mr. Torres: (*Turns and speaks to a Communication Disorders department intern.*) She keeps saying *pom*. I don't know what she means.

Intern: She's saying *farm*. Sally nearly always substitutes the *p* sound for the *f* sound. For example, she'll say *pish* for *fish* and *pun* for *fun*.

Mr. Torres: You're right! She does do that.

Intern: When you hear Sally say *pom* for *farm*, acknowledge what she has said by repeating *farm* and stretching out the *f* sound so it's more noticeable to her. Say it like this: *fffffffarm*.

Mr. Torres: Should I do this every time or just sometimes?

Intern: Model as often as you can without taking away from the communication interaction. Make sure that Sally still feels that you are listening to what she says and not just how she says it. You can also have Sally focus on your mouth as you produce the *f* sound in *farm*. Put your finger up to your lower lip as if you are pointing at your top teeth, touching your lower lip as you make the *f* sound. This will help Sally see how to make the sound correctly.

The communication skills of toddlers (and preschoolers) vary considerably across age spans and from child to child. Speech and language development is affected by many factors, including age, prior experiences with language, the child's health, and the home environment (Galinsky 2010). Speech and language delays affect up to eight percent of preschool children, often persist into the school years, and are sometimes associated with lowered school performance and behavior problems (Berkman et al. 2015).

When teachers like Mrs. Taylor are on their own, these delays can be difficult to identify and address. All teachers should have access to supports, like Mr. Torres does. The intern, a student in a communication disorders program at a nearby university, is studying to be a speech-language pathologist. She assists Mr. Torres in identifying Sally's speech pattern, increasing Mr. Torres's ability to understand and teach Sally.

Working with a Speech-Language Pathologist

Speech-language pathologists can help teachers understand which communication behaviors are typical for a particular age range and which ones indicate a need for assessment and possibly an intervention. Sally's substitution of *p* for *f* is not a cause for concern since she is not yet 3 years old—but it would be concerning if she were 4. Still, Sally will benefit from having Mr. Torres and the intern model correct sound pronunciation to enhance her speech development.

Becoming Partners

This article was sparked by a collaborative experience between an Early Head Start center and the Communication Disorders department at Truman State University, in Kirksville, Missouri. The Early Head Start programs in northeast Missouri bring children to the university's Speech and Hearing Clinic to receive speech-language-hearing screenings. Head Start requires screenings to be conducted within 45 days of enrollment. In addition, screenings are conducted at least annually—and more frequently if a child is suspected of having a developmental delay.

To more effectively serve children and families, Early Head Start administrators and Communication Disorders faculty agreed to increase the involvement of interns and faculty at the Early Head Start center. To ensure a mutually beneficial partnership, they decided that

- Two or more seniors or master's students (interns) in the Communication Disorders department would provide speech-language enrichment services to children in the Early Head Start center
- Interns would be selected by the university faculty, with final approval by representatives from Early Head Start
- Interns would be supervised on- and off-site by Communication Disorders department faculty
- Early Head Start staff would work collaboratively with Communication Disorders department interns and faculty to establish a working schedule and to provide a suitable space to conduct speech-language enrichment sessions
- Early Head Start staff would communicate with Communication Disorders department interns and faculty on a routine basis to review the objectives, specific goals, strengths, and weaknesses of the speech-language enrichment program

What Do Speech-Language Pathologists Do?

Speech-language pathologists evaluate, diagnose, and treat communication-based concerns about children and adults, including issues related to voice and articulation, language, fluency (stuttering), and hearing and auditory processing. They also serve individuals with autism spectrum disorder, swallowing disorders, cleft lip and palate, and neurological disorders. Speech-language pathologists work with clients across the life span in a variety of different settings—such as schools, hospitals, private clinics, and rehabilitation centers—and work collaboratively with many other professionals, such as teachers, physical and occupational therapists, physicians, and audiologists.

In practice, two Communication Disorders department interns, under the direct supervision of a faculty member (a licensed and certified speech-language pathologist), worked at the Early Head Start center two days a week for 15 weeks; their goal was to reduce the risk of speech and language problems in children ages 15 to 36 months. Interns, the faculty supervisor, teachers, staff, and parents worked together to enhance the speech-language learning environment for the children.

The interns led the children in language-based activities, often by asking open-ended questions, and used the following language-enriching techniques:

- **Modeling and reinforcement**—Demonstrating the use of vocabulary and grammatical structures, and offering specific praise when those models are imitated
  - Example—Intern models a two-word utterance containing an adjective and a noun: "Happy baby." Young child repeats, "Happy baby." Intern responds with excitement: "Yes, happy baby!"
- **Expansion**—Adding semantic and syntactic details to incomplete utterances
  - Example—Young child says, "Baby crying." Intern says, "The baby is crying," expanding the child's two words into a complete sentence.
- **Extension**—Adding information to a child's comment
  - Example—Young child says, "The baby is crying." Intern responds by saying, "The baby is crying. He is telling his mommy that he is hungry."

The interns also conducted an in-service program that showed the teachers and staff how to use these techniques.

To further the interns' education and ensure the children received high-quality support, the supervising faculty member often joined in to demonstrate appropriate interactions and techniques with the children. The faculty member also provided written feedback to the interns and met with them each week to talk about the previous week's sessions and to plan for the coming week.

Collaborating with Teachers

A number of research studies have shown that in the context of the preschool classroom, children's language development can be improved through targeted interventions (Pence, Justice, & Wiggins 2008; Wasik, Bond, & Hindman 2006). When teachers and speech-language pathologists work collaboratively to facilitate early communication development, the likelihood of delays and disorders of speech and language may be minimized (Dinnebeil, Pretti-Frontczak, & McInerney 2008). Early identification of communication difficulties in children can prevent the development of other problems, such as challenging behavior, learning difficulties (especially in reading and spelling), and social and emotional issues.

There are many ways speech-language pathologists or, as in our partnership with the Early Head Start center, interns supported by a speech-language pathologist can collaborate with early childhood teachers. They can

- Help teachers understand what is typical (that is, within the normal range) for speech and language development among children of different ages and what might be cause for concern.
- Support teachers in modifying their language output to increase children's comprehension and facilitate children's expressive language development. The language children are exposed to is a critical factor in children's own language output (Dickinson & McCabe 2001; Wasik, Bond, & Hindman 2006). As a rule of thumb, teachers should aim to speak with each child using language that is slightly more advanced than the child's. (But if a child seems to have difficulty understanding, then teachers should simplify their speech, as needed.)

- Example of supporting expressive language development—If a toddler holding a ball says, "Mine," the teacher may respond with, "Yes, that is your ball," and then pick up another ball and say, "This ball is mine." Over the coming days and weeks, the teacher may intentionally create opportunities to use the words *mine* and *yours* with the child.

› Deepen teachers' knowledge of what to focus on, when to engage, and how to enhance children's communication. Strategies such as modeling, repeating, and providing ample wait time for children to respond can be helpful.

- Example of modeling—Use self-talk or parallel talk. A teacher may engage in *self-talk* (which is like thinking out loud) when building a tower with a toddler by saying, "Block on," as she adds a block. The teacher may use *parallel talk* (describing what the child is doing) while observing or playing with the child by cheerfully exclaiming, "You knocked down the tower!," as the child knocks over the blocks.

- Example of repeating—A child says *dut* for *duck,* and the teacher repeats *duck*, emphasizing the *k* at the end of the word. Repeating is particularly useful when highlighting specific sounds that a child pronounces incorrectly.

› Encourage teachers to ask more open-ended questions. Closed questions like, "What is that?," typically have only one correct answer. In contrast, open questions like, "What do you want to play?," have more than one acceptable answer and are often good conversation starters. Questions that offer a choice are particularly useful with children who are exerting their independence—for example, "Do you want corn or peas?"

› Remind teachers to talk frequently and to use varied vocabulary and sentence structures. *Event casting*—providing an ongoing description of an activity or an event (like sportscasting)—is a great technique for teachers to use with toddlers. For example, during lunch the teacher might begin event casting with, "Sally is eating peas with a spoon. Johnny is eating turkey with a fork."

No matter which techniques teachers prefer, their goal should be a language-rich learning environment. Research shows that the quantity and quality of the conversations adults have with children impact their language learning (Garstein, Crawford, & Robertson 2008; Hart & Risley 1999).

Supporting Families

To maximize the impact of our partnership with the Early Head Start center, the interns communicated in writing and face-to-face with parents and other family members. At the end of each week, they sent home a written summary of the week's activities. The summaries contained activities that families could complete together to enhance their children's speech and language development. An example of a weekly summary is provided on page 122.

Week 3 Lesson Summary: Body Parts

Objective

After completing this week's lesson, children will point to at least five individual body parts. Children will say and/or repeat the targeted body part when prompted in at least three of five opportunities.

Targeted Vocabulary

Nose, eyes, mouth, ears, head

Shoulder, arm, hand, finger

Leg, knee, foot, ankle, toes

Classroom Activities

Two main activities will be repeatedly used in the classroom:

Sticker activity—Working from the list of targeted vocabulary, an intern will place a sticker on a body part and, at the same time, name the body part. The intern will then place a sticker on the child's corresponding body part and ask, "Where's the sticker?" The activity will continue, addressing each body part on the vocabulary list.

Body part song —The intern will sing the body part song (to the tune of "Where Is Thumbkin?"). They will encourage the children to sing along and to identify their own body parts when they are named in the song.

Activities to Try at Home

Getting dressed—As you help your child dress in the morning, name their body parts. For example, while helping your child put on a shirt, say, "Arm," while touching their arm. Or if your child can say more than one word, model a phrase like "arm in shirt."

Simon Says—Play Simon Says with your child, using the targeted body part vocabulary. For example, "Simon Says . . . touch your nose." Children enjoy doing what Simon says and playing Simon by giving directions to family members.

In addition, interns offered to meet with parents and other caregivers to discuss the goals of the speech-language enrichment sessions, to explain their children's current abilities, and to demonstrate activities that were conducted in the classroom and suggested for use at home.

Conclusion

Classroom-based collaboration between speech-language pathologists and teachers is a promising means of facilitating speech and language development in young children. Partnerships between early childhood classrooms and university programs can benefit all parties, offering additional services to children, professional development for teachers, and practice for interns. Such collaboration can promote consistent sharing of ideas and information grounded in the expertise of professional teachers and speech-language pathologists to enhance young children's communication skills. Teachers and speech-language pathologists bring unique strengths to the collaborative relationship, and effective collaboration will result in greater communication success for young children and interns alike. As one intern commented, "This was an amazing experience that provided for meaningful interactions with teachers, children, and families; encouraged collaboration with others; and resulted in substantial learning through supported practice and constructive feedback."

REFERENCES

Berkman, N.D., I. Wallace, L. Watson, T. Coyne-Beasley, K. Cullen, C. Wood, & K.N. Lohr. 2015. *Screening for Speech and Language Delays and Disorders in Children Age 5 Years or Younger: A Systematic Review for the US Preventive Services Task Force*. Report. Rockville, MD: Agency for Healthcare Research and Quality. www.ncbi.nlm.nih.gov/books/NBK305676.

Dickinson, D.K., & A. McCabe. 2001. "Bringing It All Together: The Multiple Origins, Skills, and Environmental Supports of Early Literacy." *Learning Disabilities Research & Practice* 16 (4): 186–202.

Dinnebeil, L., K. Pretti-Frontczak, & W. McInerney. 2008. "A Consultative Itinerant Approach to Service Delivery: Considerations for the Early Childhood Community." *Language, Speech, and Hearing Services in Schools* 40 (4): 435–45.

Galinsky, E. 2010. *Mind in the Making: The Seven Essential Life Skills Every Child Needs*. New York: HarperCollins.

Garstein, M.A., J. Crawford, & C.D. Robertson. 2008. "Early Markers of Language and Attention: Mutual Contributions and the Impact of Parent–Infant Interactions." *Child Psychiatry and Human Development* 39 (1): 9–26.

Hart, B., & T.R. Risley. 1999. *The Social World of Children Learning to Talk*. Baltimore: Brookes.

Pence, K.L., L.M. Justice, & A.K. Wiggins. 2008. "Preschool Teachers' Fidelity in Implementing a Comprehensive Language-Rich Curriculum." *Language, Speech, and Hearing Services in Schools* 39 (3): 329–41.

Wasik, B.A., M.A. Bond, & A. Hindman. 2006. "The Effects of a Language and Literacy Intervention on Head Start Children and Teachers." *Journal of Educational Psychology* 98 (1): 63–74.

Reflection Questions

1. How do you assess language and communication skills in your classroom? Based on those observations or other data, what strategies and techniques do you use to embed language development opportunities in your curriculum and everyday routines?
2. What professionals in your community, such as speech-language pathologists, resource specialists in early learning programs or schools, or supports at a local college or university, could collaborate with you to support children's language and communication skills?
3. How can you work with families to support children's language and communication skills?
4. Think of a few different interactions you've recently engaged in with the children you teach. With a colleague or other partner, practice enriching children's language and communication skills with the three techniques discussed in the article (modeling and reinforcement, expansion, and extension).

About the Author

Janet L. Gooch, PhD, CCC-SLP, is chancellor of the University of Illinois Springfield. She is an American Speech Language-Hearing Association-accredited and state-licensed speech-language pathologist.

Index

Page numbers followed by *b*, *f*, and *t* indicate boxes, figures, and tables, respectively.